Ray W. Pierson

Giving and Growing

Giving and Growing

Finance and Public Relations in the Local Church

Margaret F. Donaldson

FLEMING H. REVELL COMPANY

Printed in the United States of America

LIBRARY OF CONGRESS CARD CATALOG NUMBER 56-10892

Westwood, N.J.—316 Third Avenue
London E. C. 4—29 Ludgate Hill
Glasgow C. 2—229 Bothwell Street

CONTENTS

PART II Reaching Three Publics

PART III The Church Budget

PREFACE

Many profound things are being said these days on the subject of public relations. But all the definitions boil down to this: good public relations is the combination of appearance, personality, and character which attracts, holds, and enriches people.

Appearance, personality, character.

If you question the order of importance of those qualities, consider the matter for a moment.

Your neighbor may have a sterling character and a heart of gold—but if his personality is blank, you're not apt to stay with him long enough to appreciate his character.

He may have a sparkling, magnetic personality, but if he habitually needs a shave and has soup spots on his shirt—that's enough for you.

If it's true of people, it's true of churches.

The appearance attracts you. The personality holds you. The character enriches you.

It is to be regretted that the words "good public relations" are sometimes used to denote superficial gestures of good will—a kindness with which you hope to curry favor, a box of candy to somebody's secretary. There is a danger that the term may acquire the connotation of the word "politician."

Let us be sure we understand that church public relations is not a hollow technique for winning friends and increasing membership. It should be regarded as an indispensible instrument for leading people to the eternal, spiritual resources which the church makes available to them; a means of helping turn their minds and hearts toward God.

This book does not delve into the philosophical implications of public relations or the subtle ways in which the art manifests itself. Other volumes have done this, and have done it adequately. It does not offer a documented defense of the use of public relations techniques in the field of religion. We take it for granted that no such defense is necessary.

We are attempting to make a practical approach to a workable public relations program, and to show the effect it can have upon a church.

Heartfelt thanks go to the Rev. Everett F. Hallock for opening the door to the writing of this book, and to the Rev. Edgar N. Jackson for leading the author through it. Deep appreciation is also due Mrs. Irene Albers for patient cooperation in the preparation of the manuscript.

Margaret F. Donaldson

Mamaroneck, N.Y.

PART I

Church Public Relations

Chapter I

Appearance: *Attracting People*

The next time you take a motor trip, stop on the far side of some town along the way and ask the occupants of the car what they noticed as they rode through. They'll tell you about two or three gas stations, a supermarket or shopping center, a real estate office, Joe's Bar and Grill, a diner. Someone *might* have noticed a church, but if you ask him what denomination it was, the chances are he will not know. He didn't see the sign.

The bulletin-board type of church sign was designed back in the horse and buggy days when people drove past a church—or walked past—slowly enough to turn their heads and scrutinize the words. It is incredible that churches are still depending upon them for identification.

In this day of fast highway travel, bulletin boards are completely worthless as attention-getters. They are practically worthless as information-givers. If you really want to know the name of a church, you have to park your car, walk across the lawn, part the ivy, and peer through a pane of glass.

Why did your passengers know there were gas stations, supermarkets, real estate firms, and taverns in town? Because the signs hung near the street with the frank intention of arresting people.

Every church should have at least three signs: first and most essential, the identifying double-faced sign perpendicular to the highway; then an informational bulletin board, legible and carefully placed for persons who really want to know the name of the minister and the time of services; finally a directional sign pointing to the church from important street intersections or along the highway announcing that the church is a mile or two miles ahead.

A skeptical layman asks, "Do you mean you expect people to stop their cars and come into a church just because they see a sign?"

That, of course, is the ultimate goal of every phase of a good public relations program. But the immediate purpose of a sign is to attract the attention of the passer-by and to build in his mind the strong impression of an endless succession of churches—every one of which is eager to welcome him into its sanctuary.

Not every automobile driver who sees an Ajax gasoline sign turns in *immediately* to fill his tank. It might not be a convenient time. Perhaps he doesn't need gasoline at that moment. He may not use Ajax at all. But get out in front of him with enough of those Ajax signs and he'll soon be convinced that it's a brand of high quality. One day, when he is running low, he'll drive in to fill his tank with the gas that has caught his attention most frequently and most favorably.

No matter what it costs to erect the kind of sign which draws attention to your church, it is well worth the expenditure. But there is no reason to take it for granted that the cost will be prohibitive. When a sign must be anchored to an iron framework in an exterior wall, it is of course a job for professional workmen. But in a suburban or rural congregation, surely there are skillful carpenters and painters who can build a standard twelve or fourteen feet high with a hanging panel. The principal expense is the cost of the lumber, paint and braces; the lettering, which should be done by a professional sign painter; and the cement for the anchorage.

A city church with a minimum set-back from the curb often encounters difficulties because of ordinance restrictions. The first job of the public relations committee is to find out just what the municipal ordinance permits: how large a sign can be, how far it can overhang. Then make the most conspicuous use of the legal space available.

It is an illuminating experience to watch pedestrians pass a city church. How many glance at the sign? How many stop to read it? How many ignore it completely? Call a public relations committee meeting sometime in a car parked at the curb and try to figure out how your sign could attract more attention.

This was done in front of a prominent New York City church, and it was discovered that the sign was placed at a bad angle; it was too high, the lettering too small and the message was not sufficiently cogent. When these faults were corrected, the committee met in the car again. Unfortunately no statistics were compiled, but the members agree heartily that there was a noticeable difference in the reaction of pedestrians. Even passers-by who were obviously not of that church's faith were attracted by the sign.

Incidentally, that committee and the minister were surprised to discover that the name of the church did not appear on the first sign at all! It is carved in stone high above the church's door—but how many persons crane their necks to look up at that? That omission was corrected when the sign was changed.

A church located at the intersection of two heavily traveled highways has a special problem. A hanging sign may be seen from east and west—but what about traffic approaching from north and south? The solution is either to have two signs—one on each side of the corner—or a three-faced sign on the lawn at angles which will command notice from every direction. The committee will have to walk and drive toward the church from all approaches to decide upon the most effective way to identify a corner church.

On an identifying sign, lettering should be kept to a minimum:

ST. JOHN'S
LUTHERAN
CHURCH

or

THE
PRESBYTERIAN
CHURCH

The words on the bulletin board should be as few as possible. If it contains a message, it should be terse. If it cannot be read at a glance, it is either ignored or it becomes a traffic hazard.

To an alert public relations committee, the following advice is superfluous—but travel around the country on a Monday morning and you'll realize how badly the advice is needed: the Sunday sermon topic should never remain on the bulletin board for Monday's sun to shine on. A church should certainly be as careful about an outdated program as a movie house or theater.

When new letters are ordered for a bulletin board, a completely new supply should be obtained. When a well-worn alphabet is supplemented instead of replaced, a motley collection of tan, beige, and white letters shows up on the sign.

There are several sources of ideas for succinct bulletin board messages, and one of the best is the Bible. A portion of a verse of Scripture can be a quick challenge to the imagination.

"GAVE HE POWER TO BECOME"
"I WILL GIVE YOU REST"
"WHATSOEVER YE SHALL ASK, BELIEVING"
"MY PEACE I GIVE UNTO YOU"
"I HAVE OVERCOME THE WORLD"
"MOUNT UP WITH WINGS AS EAGLES"

Members of the public relations committee might submit their own suggestions—but they should always be thought-provoking and in good taste.

The Religion in American Life theme is usually suited to bulletin board use: "Give Them a Faith to Live By," or "Worship Together This Week."

Someone other than the minister should take care of bulletin board changes. The custodian, a responsible Boy Scout, or a member of the public relations committee can well undertake that task. It is as undignified for a clergyman to do it as it is to have him scrubbing the steps or hanging out the wash.

Once your signs have been installed, they should attract attention around the clock—not just in the daytime. Most bulletin boards have interior lighting—and this should be as bright as possible. But to illuminate the high, identifying sign, well-placed spotlights may be concealed at the base or in nearby shrubbery. Two spotlights can burn six hours at a cost of approximately twelve cents.

A third type of sign essential for every church is a directional sign placed at the city limits or at busy intersections. In a small community in northeastern New York State, you pass two churches on a major highway route. It is impossible to see the names of those churches at a glance. At one corner, however, there is a large arrow attached to a pole and it reads: "Episcopal Church—three blocks." Few travelers ever see that church—but they know it is there. If anyone can pass through your town without knowing your church is there, your signs are not doing their job!

Before installing a conspicuous sign in front of your church, take a long objective look at the building and property and ask yourself if you really *want* to call attention to it.

Does it need a coat of paint? Are there rust stains under the hinges or around the window sills? Are the steps clean? Are there any cracked windows? Is the shrubbery carefully tended and the grass neatly manicured? Is the property free of papers and refuse? Are the walks and driveways in good repair? Study it as though you were a stranger seeing it for the first time. Maybe you'll want to take your signs down so passers-by won't notice it at all!

It may be seen, right here, how the public relations committee overlaps other church committees. At this point it is the property committee whose chairman should have a thorough understanding of the vital role the church's appearance plays in attracting the favorable attention of the public.

The public relations workers and the trustees should join forces to keep a vigilant eye on property adjacent to or near the church. First of all, is it possible to purchase property for future expansion or for parking and playground space—or to protect the church from undesirable business or industry?

Zoning Boards are required to notify property owners within a certain radius when a hearing is to be held on a zoning change or an appeal for a variance. There are many sad cases where the notice was ignored—as was the legal ad in the newspaper—and the Zoning Board granted an undesirable change which vigorous protest from members of the church might have prevented.

One of the most important matters on the permanent agenda of the public relations committee is that of *custodial service*. Here, again, the committee must work not only in cooperation with the property committee but also with the finance committee.

In a moderate-sized church, what are the duties of the custodian? Is he just the bell-ringer? Is he expected only to cut the grass, shovel snow, keep the floors and carpets clean, and run the dish washer?

Those duties are important, of course. But not until the custodian's status as the Number One public relations officer is recognized will a church be confident about the impression it makes upon strangers.

A good custodian, in addition to being an efficient and tireless housekeeper, must also be a gardener, a carpenter, a painter, an electrician, a plumber, and a mechanic. If he is not such a multi-talented man, then he should be given assistance, so that every one of these services is covered.

In a city church, there is the added task of keeping constant watch over the sidewalk and steps at twenty-minute intervals to be sure that the area is free from refuse.

Is anyone asking, "Why all this emphasis on appearance?" Do the externals really matter so much? Jesus had no custodian. In fact, He had no church. People gathered in the fields or on the beach or along the streets to hear Him.

The answer surely is obvious. The principal function of a church, as that of any structure, is to shelter people. We want protection from the elements, and a quiet place away from noisy distractions to worship God.

We have no apology for constructing buildings for that purpose. And since we have buildings, their cleanliness and beauty reflect our love and respect for the function those buildings serve.

Ask again, "Why this emphasis upon appearance—" and let us answer it with another question. When you see a slovenly, ill-kempt man, what do you know about him? You know, first of all, that he has very little self-esteem. He has no interest in attracting people. He cannot expect you to have more respect for him than he has for himself.

When you pass a slovenly, run-down church, what does it tell you about the members and the minister?

The same thing, unfortunately.

Let us assume that your church is clearly identified, that the building is freshly painted—or, if it is of stone or brick construction, that the exterior is clean and in good repair. The property is neat and well kept. Strong floodlights illuminate the structure every night. In short, it shows evidence of the love and respect of a devoted congregation.

A stranger wakes up one Sunday morning and says, "Let's go to church today."

"All right—where shall we go?" asks his wife.

"Let's go to that good-looking Congregational church."

So you have caught his attention. He is arrested.

Now what happens when he goes inside?

Chapter II

Personality: *Holding People*

The personality of the church begins to manifest itself as soon as a stranger steps over the threshold. If he is greeted with a firm handshake and a cordial "good morning" from a pleasant, well-groomed usher, he knows he is welcome. If he is aware of a friendly spirit around him as the people gather for the service, he feels relaxed and comfortable.

As he reads the bulletin, he learns many things about the church. He knows if the minister is being deprived of office assistance or needs a new typewriter or new duplicating equipment. He knows how much of a premium is placed on neatness, economy of expression, accurate spelling, good grammar, alert proof reading.

A sampling of bulletins from churches of various sizes is a discouraging experience. It is possible to mimeograph a bulletin which, for legibility, neatness, and attractiveness of layout, cannot be surpassed by a commercial printer. But let us hasten to add that a faultless mimeographed bulletin is rare. Some of the materials placed in parishioners' hands on Sunday morning should have been consigned to the wastebasket in the church office. It is far better to hear announcements from the pulpit than to peer at a smudged, illegible, badly composed bulletin. It is incredible that a clergyman who would not tolerate an usher in a dirty shirt or an organist who repeatedly strikes wrong notes, will allow a bulletin in the sanctuary that is in the same category.

Let us here make a plea for *printed* bulletins, for all but the very smallest churches. Don't say you can't afford it before you have read Part III of this book, on expanding the budget!

One church inaugurated the use of printed bulletins by offering them as memorials. A committee of ten women was organized, each to obtain three other persons who would pay for the printing one Sunday out of the year, in memory of a loved one. Each bulletin carried an inscription like this: "The bulletin today is given by Mrs. John Smith in memory of her father, Samuel Jones."

The list repeated itself year after year as birthdays or anniversaries came around. Each donor paid five dollars. As the years passed, the printer's price went up and an amount was placed in the budget to supplement the memorial gifts.

If the bulletin is mimeographed, there are several details which should command vigilance. The very best grade of paper should be used to prevent the words from showing through. The typewriter type should be brushed clean to avoid "filled" letters. If the office typewriter is old, look up a good one in someone's office or home and type the stencil there.

At the end of this book is a list of suggestions for turning out an attractive, legible bulletin.

Books of sketches, religious symbols, and unusual lettering for headlines are available from mimeo supply companies. There is a danger, however, in getting "sketch happy" and cluttering up the pages of your bulletin with too many illustrations. The material should always be chosen with the dignity of the church in mind.

Every bulletin should include the name of the church and the name of the minister. Unnecessary advice? You'd be surprised at the number of "anonymous" ones! Care should always be exercised at the folding of the bulletin; even a Sunday school class (which has the job in some churches) can be taught to match the edges perfectly before making the crease.

There is probably no wider area of deviation among churches than in the handling of the ushering problem. Whether the church is a large one with two dozen ushers at each service impeccably dressed and trained—or a rural church where two willing men are recruited at the beginning of the service, it is a significant factor in the public relations program. When ushers are improperly dressed, walk in a slovenly manner, talk to each other during the service, seat persons at the wrong time, cause disturbances with doors and windows, they can shatter the worshipful atmosphere of a service.

Paul E. Allison, head usher at a church in Bloomington, Illinois, has this to say on the subject:

> * The ushers are the direct representatives of the church to the public. Visitors receive their first impression of the church from the ushers, who should convey a kind and friendly attitude of a church deserving of their respect and support.
>
> The nominating committee should exercise great care in the selection of the ushering committee, of which the

* From *Methodist Action*, January, 1955.

chairman is the head usher. The head usher must have complete authority to select ushers to serve for a definite term, at the end of which they are asked to serve again or are replaced.

The head usher should be a church member in good standing, a good organizer, and a natural leader. Other ushers should be selected primarily on the basis of Christian character and ability. Let it be understood that ushers are a picked group of men who have an important office.

The worshiper should be greeted at the door, made to feel welcome, taken to a seat and given a church bulletin. The period before the start of the service should be dignified and with as little fanfare as possible. A simple "Good morning" is better than a hand shake, unless offered by the visitor.

Following the service, the attitude of the usher should be more informal. He should greet people by name, shake hands, perhaps inquire about the family, and record the names and addresses of visitors for the pastor and church office. Last impressions are lasting impressions and in some respects how a congregation is dismissed is more important than how it is received.

The worshipfulness of the service can be increased by filling the front seats first and then moving towards the back. By this plan worshipers are not distracted by seating persons in front of them, vacant seats are at the back for those who are late, and the sanctuary has the appearance of fullness to everyone.

Filling the front first is made easier if the rear two-thirds of the pews are closed off with a ribbon which has a weight attached to the front end and can be moved back one row at a time until either the room is full or everyone is seated. This procedure will not be very popular at first, but as the reason becomes apparent, the congregation will cooperate in a fine spirit.

The mechanics of taking up the collection vary as to size and shape of the sanctuary, although the same principles apply as for a sanctuary with center aisle and straight, equal length pews. The ushers assemble in the rear foyer, go down the center aisle two abreast, spread out before the altar for the plates or prayers, and then take their places, divided between center and outside aisles, working back in orderly fashion.

. . . . .

Ushers should wear similarity of suits, depending upon the season, but it need not be formal. Never should an usher appear in a sport shirt or without a coat. A flower in the lapel, whether artificial or genuine, adds much to the appearance, and distinguishes him as an usher.

Never should an usher smell of tobacco or of anything that might prove offensive to the worshiper. He should stand erect and not slouch or lean against the walls and pews. There should be no long conversations among the ushers or with the head usher. . . .

The University of Omaha, School of Adult Education, has prepared an excellent correspondence course for the church usher which would be profitable for the head usher. A booklet such as *Church Ushering* by Paul H. D. Lang should be read by every new usher. Only by such preparation can a man properly serve his church in such an important office.

We left our stranger some time ago waiting for the service to begin. He now has a definite feeling about the personality of the church from his initial greeting, from the appearance of the sanctuary, and from his perusal of the bulletin. The impression is further strengthened by the bearing of the minister in the pulpit, by the smoothness and dignity of the order of service, by the excellence of the music.

Nothing can blast a service with such devastation as inferior music, and no subject is quite so "touchy" from the public relations point of view. There is good reason for that. Music is often produced by conscientious, hard-working volunteers whose years of service and sacrifice have built a protective bulwark against criticism.

When a soloist or organist or choir director has served long past his period of usefulness, it is clear that replacements must be made and it is time for the public relations and music committees to decide what to do.

Just as there is no law which requires a church to have a bulletin, there is no law which says there *must* be a choir or a soloist. In order to keep hurt feelings to a minimum, it sometimes proves advisable to dispense with a choir and soloists for a year and have only organ music. Guest organists might be brought in from time to time to play the offertory. A new choir can eventually be developed.

There are many ways to handle such a situation with tact. But if there finally proves to be no way of solving the problem without hurting a faithful volunteer, the music committee must have the courage to do it as painlessly as possible. Offending—or even causing the withdrawal of one person or a few persons, as much as we deplore it, is far less of an evil than to ruin a worship service for several hundred persons.

If the stranger is aware of the personality of the church at a worship service, he becomes increasingly impressed as he takes part in the activities of the organizations. If he is made to feel at home, given worthwhile jobs to do, assimilated into the educational or social program, he soon feels a closeness and warmth which binds him to the church as to a good friend.

There are five ways in which the personality of a church can be felt in a community.

One is the frequency and thoroughness with which its activities are reported in the newspapers. If a church takes full advantage of every opportunity for publicity, it not only informs its members and friends about what is going on; it also establishes a reputation as an alert, wide-awake institution with a vigorous constituency and a fruitful program.

The whole topic of newspaper coverage will be handled in a subsequent chapter, and is therefore being passed over here with only a sharp indication of its importance as a public relations tool.

A second way in which a community becomes aware of the vitality of a church is through surveys undertaken from time to time to determine the religious leanings of the population. Parish visitation is a necessity—but so also is the outreach into new housing developments and apartment houses where an effort is made to locate and interest potential members. No matter what the faith of a newcomer is, he is favorably impressed by a caller at the door who says, "I am from the First Baptist Church and we have been wondering whether you are of the Protestant faith. If you haven't any affiliation, we would like to invite you to visit us." He then hands the resident a card or leaflet which announces the time of the services and lists the organizations in the church.

If the answer is, "We are Roman Catholics" or "We are Jewish" or "We are Methodists," the caller thanks him for the information and says, "That's a very active congregation and we are sure you will feel at home there."

As the new resident closes the door, he is sure to think, "Those Baptists are certainly on the job!"

A third way to reach into the community is through the use of questionnaires which guide the minister and officials in their planning of the religious and social program. If people attend your church for a time and then stop coming, you should know why they stop. If they have needs which are not being met by the church, that is vital information for the minister to have. Many clergymen are also interested in suggestions for sermon topics. The worship committee should be anxious for ideas for the improvement of the order of service. What attracted a newcomer to your church? What is it that keeps him coming? The way to find out is to ask him.

An excellent guide for the compilation of such questionnaires and their distribution may be found in Willard Pleuthner's valuable books, *Building Up Your Congregation* and *More Power For Your Church*. (See Books on Publicity and Public Relations, p. 151.)

Another vital way in which a community becomes aware of a church is through special services for organizations such as the Boy Scouts, veterans' groups, firemen, etc. If the church doors are open also to meetings of secular or service clubs, it gains a reputation for hospitality.

Many persons who have come into a church for the first time to attend Community Chest or Garden Club meetings learn to feel at home there and eventually find their way to the front door on a Sunday morning.

Perhaps the most important way of all in which a church impresses the community is through the members themselves. How do you talk about your church in the presence of outsiders? How do you refer to your clergyman? What is your attitude toward the work you do?

Remember this: you represent your church to the people who associate with you. No word of destructive criticism should ever be heard from you. If you don't like your pastor or don't approve of his sermons, keep it to yourself. If you can't work happily on a committee, get off of it. A disgruntled person who says, "I've done nothing but peel potatoes in that church all year" or "I've been hooked again to teach a Sunday school class" is doing his church serious harm. There is one job every member of a church has whether he realizes it or not. He is a member of the public relations committee in the deepest sense of the term. Through his words and attitudes, the community sees either an apathetic church with a dull program or an active, growing church happily dedicated to the service of God.

Chapter III

Character: *The Enrichment of People*

So far we have a clearly identified, fine-looking building; a friendly organization whose members are occupied with a well-conducted program. It could be a school, a service club, or a fraternity.

But right here we encounter that priceless ingredient that we refer to as "character"; and at the point where the institution reaches into men's souls to forge a relationship with God, we have a church.

Here is public relations at its profoundest level and here, oddly enough, is where the public relations committee as such abdicates and transfers its function to the clergyman and to those responsible for spiritual development. The public relations experts can attract people and it can hold them. Only the minister, however, and the committee on worship or its equivalent can insure the enrichment of their lives.

When everything has been said about cleanliness, dignity, good music, comfortable pews, dedicated ushers, good lighting, adequate heating, and neat bulletins—we all know where the manna really grows. There are preachers who can inspire such spiritual resurgence that we would gladly sit on hard benches in a badly lighted, damp barn to hear them. Worshipers on their knees on a stone floor can find God without any preacher at all.

After all, what is the function of a church?

"The Christian Church is to proclaim the Gospel, the 'good news' that man is saved from sin and despair by responding to the will God made known in Jesus Christ. It is to provide a fellowship of believers, which is the Body of Christ, whose members derive their life from the one living Head, through worship and good works. It is to extend the life of Christ into every aspect of the world's life and thus becomes the instrument of the coming of the Kingdom of God on earth." (*Methodism Looks at the City* edited by Robert A. McKibben, Superintendent, Department of City Work, Division of National Missions, The Methodist Church.)

Most of us will agree that the responsibility for the salvation and spiritual nourishment of the people lies with the spiritual leader.

In many churches, the clergyman can fulfill his function adequately by preaching, by counseling, and by visiting in the homes of his parishioners. In others, however, those who study closely the spiritual development of the parish recognize a need for augmenting the preaching, counseling, and visitation of the pastor.

How can this be done?

Obviously by gathering together groups of persons for spiritual exploration—persons who will read, study, and pray in the pursuit of truth. Dedicated laymen can always be found who will fit themselves to serve as leaders of these groups.

Members of such prayer groups testify to demonstrations of mental and physical healing, guidance received, strength restored, wisdom acquired, problems solved. Many persons who cannot be reached from the pulpit or at the communion table find God in the silence which follows quiet study and directed prayer.

The public relations committee says in effect to the spiritual leaders: "We will get them there and we will do our best to hold them. But it is up to you to enrich them and lead them to the life abundant. The character of the church is in your hands."

PART II

Reaching Three Publics

Chapter IV

Out from Under the Bushel

There are three publics with which a church seeks to establish and maintain creative relations: the church family, the potential members, the rest of the world.

Since all phases of public relations reach all three publics in some measure, it is impossible to classify the tools in three neat categories. You cannot say this outlet reaches only the members, this one only potential members, and this one only the general public. It is necessary, however, to have a specific purpose and definite audience in mind as each type of publicity is prepared.

KEEPING IN TOUCH WITH THE "FAMILY"

The Sunday bulletin and the parish paper are directed primarily to the church family. They should serve as sources of information. They should reflect the ideas of the minister and the parish leaders. They are the house organs, as it were, the internal media which foster a unity of spirit and a sense of pride.

Many churches include news items in their Sunday

bulletins and mail them each week to the members in lieu of a parish paper. Others confine their bulletins to the order of service and one-line announcements of the coming week's events.

It is important that some communication reach the homes by mail at least once a month, for if a member is absent from church for three or four Sundays, he needs not only the information but the renewed sense of identification with the institution which the parish paper gives him.

If the expense of a newspaper is considered a problem, then serious thought should be given to financing the venture with advertising revenue. If the publication is written in news style and has the appearance of a miniature news sheet, advertising can be worked into the layout in such a way that it does not offend either the eye or the mind of the reader. Advertisers should never feel that they are simply making a donation to help finance a parish paper. They should be convinced that the space is as valuable to them in proportion to the circulation as similar space would be in a secular newspaper.

It requires a hard-working group of writers and editors and prompt cooperation from the church organizations to publish an effective newspaper each month, but for stimulating the interest of the members and for affording an over-all view of the activities of the church, there is nothing which can take its place.

A parish paper should maintain a high standard of news values. If the writers will follow the principals outlined in this chapter for effective news writing, a parish paper can make interesting reading. It cannot achieve that goal if it is merely a rehash of minutes of meetings.

For instance, if a story starts, "The regular monthly meeting of St. Catherine's Guild was held Friday in the parish house with Judge John Smith as the speaker on the topic, 'Children In Our Courts,' " who wants to read it—except the person who wrote it?

On the other hand, if the story begins, " 'The church is failing in its responsibility to its young people,' Judge John Smith of the Children's Court told St. Catherine's Guild Friday at a meeting in the parish house"—you have a reader.

The headline "St. Catherine's Guild Meets" will let your eye go by. Whereas a two-liner reading, "Churches Are Seen Failing In Responsibility To Youth" forces you to read the story.

A universal fault of parish paper reporters seems to be that they are willing to tell you what a speaker talked about—but not what he said!

Many pastors keep close track of special events in the lives of their parisioners: a business promotion, a student on the dean's list, election to office, a wedding anniversary, the winning of a prize or citation, the publication of an article. A brief note on these occasions reaches the heart.

Other ministers two or three times a year send a printed card announcing a sermon or series of sermons to be preached on certain dates which they hope will open the way to deeper spiritual understanding. Occasionally sermons should be printed and distributed to the members.

The week between Christmas and New Year's is the period when some pastors write personal notes of appreciation for the service members have rendered to the church the last year.

A letter from the minister appealing for support of some

special church function is often the principal factor in its success.

These communications should be on the minister's stationery and sent in envelopes bearing the return address of the parsonage. They should be invested with a personal quality which will insure thoughtful reading. This is not accomplished if the letters are too frequent or if they merely urge support of some routine church activity. They are not "promotional" letters. They are personal letters.

To a clergyman whose schedule is crowded with sermon preparation, meetings, parish calls, counseling appointments—this may seem like a mammoth job. It is.

One of the functions of the publicity committee should be to supervise the church's schedule of mailings. If a flood of letters bearing the church's return address descends upon a home too frequently, the importance of the receipt of such mail diminishes. The parishioner is apt to defer opening it and perhaps eventually to ignore it.

From one church the following items were delivered in four days: the parish newspaper, a letter from the minister, a flyer announcing a rummage sale, the minutes of a vestry meeting, a postal card announcing a men's club meeting, and a quarterly statement from the finance committee. Relations with the public were strongly established those four days—but they were also considerably strained!

REACHING THE PROSPECTS

Potential members of the church—whether they are active prospects or occasional attendants—can also be reached with the parish bulletin or newspaper if the church has an extensive mailing list. But radio, TV, and newspaper publicity plus neighborhood penetration are more constant and effective methods of catching and holding the interest of this particular public.

Neighborhood promotion fosters a neighborly feeling —whether the area is a small segment of a large city or an entire rural community.

Let us take the A. family. The A. children are sent to Sunday school at Trinity Church because it is nearby and most of their friends go there. Mrs. A. is occasionally asked to make a cake for a food sale or attend a benefit. When her parents come to visit, she takes them there to church. Mr. A. attends regularly every Easter.

If asked, they would agree that Trinity Church is an indispensable force for good in the community. But it is possible for them to live there a dozen years with no stronger impression of the church than that.

Consider the gradual effect upon Mr. A. of an active public relations program. He hears an announcement of a Trinity Church event on the radio. He sees the clergyman participating in a panel on a TV program. He is handed a flyer announcing a concert. He notices a window display depicting a mission project. He sees well-designed posters in shop windows calling attention to a bazaar. His eye is caught by a sermon topic in a newspaper advertisement. He is repeatedly conscious of the name, Trinity Church, in the columns of his local newspaper. The children bring home mimeographed announcements and printed leaflets. He finds in his mail box a card listing the services and organization meetings. He notices the name of the church on a literature rack at the railroad station.

Over a period of months or years, he gradually becomes aware of the church as a thriving institution. He is still a long way from feeling one of the family, but perhaps without realizing it, he is becoming a distant relative. One day he receives a letter asking if he will give an hour and a half to collecting pledge cards for the church, or a call from a friend asking if he will give some advice on a property problem—and he finds himself willing to be drawn into the church through the side door.

Flyers and Posters

It is essential that the publicity committee understand that great care be exercised in the preparation of the materials which are designed to reach this vast public of potential members.

The copy for flyers should be dignified and succinct. Permission for their circulation should be obtained from the municipality. There are many methods of distributing them. They may be placed in mail boxes, handed to residents at the railroad station, left in parked cars, included in packages at supermarkets, given out on the street.

The same care should be exercised in the preparation of posters. It is advisable to have them printed if possible, but if they are done by local artists, they should have the appearance of professional work. Store windows should be chosen where they will show off to the best advantage. Avoid cluttered windows or those displaying articles not in keeping with the dignity of the church. A committee should watch its posters regularly to be sure they have not fallen over or become defaced. Remove them as soon as the event they are publicizing is over.

Many churches are provided with paper posters from denominational headquarters announcing church-wide events or causes. It is a temptation to attach them to bulletin boards with thumbtacks or tape and consider the responsibility taken care of. But with the expenditure of a few cents and a little time, such a poster can be dressed up to increase its effectiveness. Press out the creases with a warm iron and mount the paper on a large piece of cardboard whose color matches one of the colors in the poster. Outline it with tape of a contrasting color and frame it with wider tape or with a half-inch wooden molding. It will be more attractive and also more durable.

An effective poster can be made by mounting several small flyers at various angles on a large bristol board.

The Pew Rack

Why do so many churches ignore the pew racks as dispensers of public relations material? A vigilant committee will pay as careful heed to the contents of the pew racks as to the literature table at the rear of the church.

A sampling of cards and leaflets found in the pew racks of Trinity Methodist Church in Albany over a period of six months reveals the following:

1. A welcoming message:

   "We welcome all friends and visitors to our worship service, believing that in the sanctuary of God all men are at home, and in the fellowship of the Church all men are brothers. We invite you to make yourself known to the ministers and to enter regularly into our fellowship. We will appreciate it if you will fill out this card on the reverse side.

Place it on the offering plate or give it to one of the ministers or ushers. We are glad you are with us today and hope you will come again."

The reverse side contains lines for name, address and telephone number; also the following items to be checked:

That We May Serve You

I am a visitor for one Sunday
I recently moved to Albany
I am a student
.... is in .... hospital
.... is ill at home and should be visited
.... desires a call from the minister
.... desires to unite with this church
.... would like to arrange for baptism
I have moved to address below

That You May Serve Others

Would like offering envelopes
Would like to serve in the church school
Would like to help in youth program
Would like to sing in choir

2. Sunday Evening Program
   Starts, "There is plenty of activity around Trinity on a Sunday evening and there is a spot for you, too. . . ."
3. Our Church Building
   (Brief history of building)
4. A Prayer for the Church
   (Several of these)

5. Prayer is Simple

    Prayer is so simple:
    It is like quietly opening a door
    And slipping into the very presence of God—
    There in the stillness
    To listen for His voice.
    Perhaps to petition
    Or only to listen,
    It matters not;
    Just to be there
    In His presence,
    Is prayer.
    (The Open-Church Association.)

6. Prayer is Power

    (A meditation on the meaning of prayer)

7. Bookmarks containing name and address of church
8. Small booklets 2¾ by 4 inches containing recent sermons by the minister.
9. Music at Trinity

    (A description of the musical program and choirs, including times of rehearsals)

10. Bible readings for use during Lent
11. Power of Silence

    "All the great powers of nature are quiet. We do not hear the moon rise or set. We do not hear the great force of gravitation hold us to the earth. We do not hear the life-giving warmth of the sun. In nature, only the destructive forces—such as wind storms, lightning and explosions are noisy. This same law is true regarding God's 'still small voice' from which we get wisdom, comfort, and hope. It is hard to hear this in many busy homes and other places where we are subjected to the pressures and noises of today. However, we can hear God's voice in the quiet of an OPEN CHURCH. Remember you are welcome to enter our Church every day."

12. The Family Pew
    Starts, "I am the Family Pew . . . I represent man's search for God and God's search for man. . . ."
13. "For Busy People"
    (An eighteen-line exhortation to Stop, Look, and Listen)
14. Motorist's Prayer
15. Folder with complete church program itemized, including names of societies and times of meetings.

This material is printed in many colors and on various sizes of cards and leaflets. One piece of literature is never left in the pew racks more than three weeks. The racks are examined after every service to insure that the cards which remain are not defaced. The public relations committee (which includes fifteen hard-working persons) maintains correspondence with other churches in order to exchange ideas and materials and all church members are alerted to bring home samples of literature from other churches when they are visiting out of town.

One of the best sources of pew-rack material is the Open-Church Association, 58 Middle Street, Gloucester, Mass.

Radio and Television

In its zeal to bring people into church, a publicity committee often neglects valuable opportunities to take the church to the people. Radio and television are, of course, the means of doing that.

How do you get your church on the radio and television? How can you get your minister or a church leader on a program?

First of all, by having a good idea. Second, by making an appointment with a station manager, the producer of an existing program, or a member of the broadcasting and film division of your local council of churches. You can, of course, buy time, financing it either through the church treasury or a sponsor, but that method is far beyond the resources of most churches.

In generating an idea, it is important to become familiar with existing programs. There are many interview shows which would welcome a minister or a church worker with an interesting story to tell. Most commentators use unusual news items about churches. Some stations begin or close their day with a prayer by a guest clergyman.

Program participation of this kind is important, but the use of creative ideas in the development of news programs is also a valuable means of broadcasting the message of religion.

In large cities, the stations deal almost exclusively with church councils or ministers' associations in the planning of religious programs. Inferior ideas are thus screened out and over-emphasis on one denomination or faith is avoided. Before you make direct contact with a station or a producer, exhaust every possibility of working through the council. The extension and improvement of religious broadcasting is the primary function of its radio and television department.

Whether it is a council of churches or a station manager you are approaching, familiarize yourself with the policy of the station. Will it give free public service time to your church? Will it broadcast or televise church services? Will it accept a series of sermons by local ministers? Will it use news items and spot announcements? Will it consider panel discussions, counseling sessions, dramatic sketches? Will it present musical programs? Bible readings?

After you have put out this preliminary feeler, then it is time to develop your ideas and get them down in program form, either on paper or on tape. When you go to a station with a request for time, you should be armed with a sample of what you have in mind.

If you have a series of spot announcements, the commentator will appreciate it if each one is timed exactly for the number of minutes the station is willing to devote to it. If it is a news item, be sure the information is accurate and complete.

By studying the church membership, you can usually uncover human interest material for interview programs: a shut-in with an unusual hobby, a church school teacher with an interesting approach to her material, a traveler who has recently returned from a visit to a mission, an old-timer who remembers what the church was like in the horse and buggy days, a visitor with a startling story to tell, a student from another country, an architect with ultra-modern ideas on church construction.

If you are planning your own program, you might start with one of these ideas: discussion of a juvenile delinquency case by your minister and a psychiatrist, a panel composed of the minister and municipal officials on the church's responsibility for the solution of civic problems, a Bible quiz program with several alert children, personal on-the-spot counsel by the minister, Bible stories dramatized in present-day idiom. Don't neglect the programs teen-agers listen to—disc jockeys, for instance, who frequently interview young people between recordings.

The day is past when fifteen minutes of straight talking —unless by a preacher of unusual renown—is welcomed by stations. What they want is an arresting program based on an unusual idea.

Before you put your own creative ideas to work, ask yourself two questions.

What is the purpose of the program? You may want to extend your minister's influence beyond the boundaries of the parish. You may want to demonstrate ways the church can influence political or social ideas. You may want to lead people to become active Christians. You may want to show how religion can affect a man's business or profession. You may want to help people directly with their problems.

What audience do you hope to reach? Programs directed at young people call for a specific approach. You may want to talk only to yourselves. You may want to reach the vast audience of non-church goers.

Remember that if your idea and presentation does not grip the interest of the audience, you are out of the room with a flick of the listener's wrist.

Find out what is available from your denomination or from interdenominational agencies in the way of film clips, background music, or prepared programs. There are 16 mm. sound motion pictures available which might serve your purpose as well as a live program.

Assure your station that you will help build an audience for your program by publicizing it in the newspapers, by mail communication to your members, and through the church bulletin and parish paper.

Be prepared to handle the mail which will reach you as a result of the program.

The ideas, the writing, and the production of programs are limited only by the imagination and skill of the talented persons in a congregation. And the talent is there somewhere if the public relations committee will work to ferret it out.

Valuable suggestions on the subject of obtaining public service time is contained in the following advice listed by the Rev. William A. Meadows, director of radio and TV services and training for the Television, Radio and Film Commission of the Methodist Church:

1. Remember, your station, radio and/or TV, probably has had some very unhappy experiences with religious and public service broadcasters. You must prove yourself.
2. Less than two per cent of the people who go to stations asking for public service time have a definite program plan to offer.
3. The station wants to have not just a biography of the man you may be putting on; they want to know what he is going to say, and what he will do.
4. All stations want people and subject matter which is timely; some want controversial material at times, but all stations need programs of human interest.
5. You do not have a captive audience! The program must be good radio or good television.
6. Public service time is worth money. Know how much it is worth. Report it to your people!
7. Too few programs of public service time are ever appreciated. Send a letter of appreciation to all the

people closely related to your production; engineers, secretaries, etc. . . .

8. Prepare yourself to meet station personnel who usually are doing your program as an extra duty. Their time is valuable, and you should treat their time carefully. Do not cost them extra and unnecessary time and inconveniences.
9. Offer your program to the station and leave the choice and placement of it up to them.
10. Let the station people know you are depending on them and seeking to learn from them.
11. Regardless of whether you represent the Red Cross of the town you are in, or your own church, you are a public service producer: What you do can reflect on all public service programming over that station.
12. You represent all organized religion, whether you want to or not.
13. Learn the traffic of the station so you will hand the right copy to the right person, and the right props to the right person.
14. Know station personnel and their responsibilities.
15. Share public relations information with them, so that station public relations people might exploit anything worthwhile.

When a church is air-minded, the minister or any layman who plans to participate should be trained in broadcasting techniques and most churches are willing to finance a minister's attendance at a workshop for this purpose. Information about the dates and places of these workshops is available either from a denomination's broadcasting and film department or from such interdenominational agencies as the National Council of Churches Broadcasting and

Film Commission, 220 Fifth Avenue, New York 1, New York, or the National Association of Evangelicals, 542 South Dearborn, Chicago 5, Illinois.

After all, every station wants to build a large viewing or listening audience. Every church wants its ideas to reach the people. A mighty opportunity for large-scale evangelism is missed when these two factors fail to implement one another.

Be sure of one thing: there is more time available for religious broadcasting than there are good ideas to fill it!

"EVERYBODY ELSE"

The third public is arrested by many of the same media which have attracted the attention of the family and the potential members, but the phase of public relations which makes the deepest imprint on the minds of non-church goers is the mention of the church which appears in the newspapers.

Advertising

In a community where the newspapers devote a generous measure of free space to church news, it is a temptation to forego paid advertising. There are several reasons, however, why a church should look with favor on that means of calling attention to its program.

First of all, it is the only sure way of saying exactly what you want to say. News copy is usually rewritten, sometimes cut and always edited. But when you buy space, it's yours. Most newspaper stories omit the price of admission to an event and such messages as "Everybody is welcome" or "Come and bring your friends." Paid advertising space is the place for that kind of promotion.

Through the use of various sizes of display type, an ad can call attention to a sermon topic or a social event which would be lost in the small type of a news story.

When a church decides to advertise, the publicity chairman should sit down with a member of the paper's advertising staff and discuss the matter. The cost per column-inch is the first thing to find out; also what saving can be effected through a contract for the use of space over an extended period.

As soon as the church determines how much space it can use for each ad, it moves to the preparation of copy. Again the advertising man will be of inestimable help in suggesting the kind of type to use and in planning the layout. From his mat files he can provide art work such as a cross or a steeple or an arched window to give the ad interest—or he might suggest a small sketch of your church or a picture of your minister.

The possibility of joint advertising should be explored by every church not only in the interest of inter-church cooperation, but also because more space can be purchased if several churches are sharing the cost.

What does a church ad hope to accomplish? Is it an information giver or an attention getter?

If there is information to be given such as the Fall opening of Sunday school, a guest preacher, or a change in the time of the worship service, the fact should be stated as briefly as possible. Such appeals as "Come and worship with us" or "The public is invited" or "Make this your church home" clutter up a small ad and accomplish very little. If you consider your ad primarily as an attention getter, you will keep the words to a minimum and make full use of the most conspicuous ingredient a newspaper can offer—white space.

A preacher once remarked that he was through with advertising because he had never heard of anyone coming to church as the result of an ad. In a newspaper the following day, three inches were devoted to the advance announcement of a concert by Arthur Rubinstein. Across the top of the ad in bold type were the words: SOLD OUT. Rubinstein's managers had spent $150 for an ad—not to attract more people to the concert, but to intensify Rubinstein's reputation as an eminent and popular pianist.

News

Before we discuss church news, let us be sure we understand the newspaper's attitude toward it.

What is news?

The simplest answer is—what people are interested in reading. A story increases in news value in direct ratio to the number of persons interested in reading it.

A distinct difference should be recognized between publicity and news. When a person asks, "How can we get more publicity for our church?" the answer is, "By publishing leaflets and brochures, distributing posters and flyers, circulating letters, buying advertising space."

We should recognize that a newspaper is not a publicity organ. A newspaper is just what it says it is—a NEWS paper and when there is a NEWS story, the paper prints it. The publicity the church gets from the story is a by-product.

It is important to remember that the larger a paper is the more strict becomes its standard of news values—due principally to the volume and variety of news it must provide for a heterogeneous collection of readers. A minister who has had great success in placing church stories in the newspaper of a small community may find it difficult when he moves to a larger city. He should anticipate the difference and study the city papers thoroughly to see what they consider newsworthy. He should continue sending stories to them, however, on all church activities with the expectation that some of them will be used even though they may be cut or condensed.

We should assume that an editor judges a story strictly in terms of its news value and be slow to charge him with personal bias if one faith or denomination appears to receive more attention from his paper than another.

Some churches provide the papers with more news than others—sometimes because they *have* more but usually because they have an alert and skillful publicity chairman constantly on the job.

The simplicity of the organizational structure and the absence of colorful, liturgical embellishments in some churches deprive them of the opportunities other churches have for colorful newspaper stories. The picture of a bishop in a business suit with a four-in-hand tie is not as alluring to a newspaper as the picture of a bishop in eye-catching vestments. Even titles differ in color. Compare Stated Clerk or District Superintendent, for instance, with Suffragan

Bishop or Monsignor. Churches which lack drama and color need imaginative publicity writers to develop every opportunity to produce a news story.

Newspapers in large cities are usually interested in major building projects, appointments of new clergymen, large convocations involving delegates from a wide area, action taken on controversial subjects. Since these papers cover so many churches, meetings of committees or organizations are not considered news—unless a well-known speaker has something startling to say.

As for feature articles or human interest items, city papers usually welcome ideas but prefer to assign their own reporters to write the stories.

Most city papers give a brief but balanced coverage to sermons and are careful to distribute their space equitably among the various faiths over an extended period of time. If your minister has an unusually timely sermon in prospect, a résumé should be sent to the papers by Thursday of the preceding week so that the editors will have ample notice to assign a reporter to cover it if it seems of special interest.

In a small community where the newspaper welcomes a wide variety of news, the situation is entirely different. It means vigilance and hard work on the part of the publicity committee, but advance and follow-up stories should be submitted concerning every organization meeting, special service, or general church event.

In one town of 60,000 population, one of the churches had the following stories in print in one month:

1. Meeting of the woman's society.
   Two advance stories, a picture of the guest speaker,

a follow-up story, and a picture taken at the meeting.

2. One sermon résumé.
3. Two meetings of the Service Guild.
   Two advance and two follow-up stories on each.
4. Boy Scout dinner.
   One advance and one follow-up with picture.
5. Advance announcement of rummage sale.
6. Ushers' communion breakfast.
   Two advances, one follow-up.
7. Picture of mothers' group sewing for bazaar.
8. New members received.
9. Reception honoring pastor on twenty-fifth anniversary of ordination.
10. Election of three trustees.
11. Sunday school mission program.
12. Youth meetings (two groups).
    Four Monday follow-ups on each.

To insure coverage like that, every organization must have a publicity chairman and the general church publicity chairman usually checks by telephone to see that each one is doing his job before and after each meeting. Obviously, it is necessary for the general chairman to keep a full calendar of church events.

There are certain basic rules to follow in submitting news to a paper:

1. Have a brief interview with the city editor or religious editor to determine the paper's policy on church news. Do they want stories written or do they want just facts listed? Will they take a story over the telephone? What is the deadline? Will they send a photographer to take pictures? Will they print pictures

taken by the church's photographer? For pictures of speakers, do they prefer glossy prints or mats? Do they print regular notices of Sunday services free of charge?

2. When you plan to call on an editor or a reporter, telephone him first to ask when you might see him for a few minutes. Don't risk dropping in at deadline time.
3. All material should be typed double-spaced on one side of the paper only.
4. A paragraph should not be broken at the bottom of a page.
5. The name, address, and telephone number of the person submitting a story should appear at the top.
6. At least two inches should be left blank at the top of each page. Don't write headlines.
7. Names must be spelled correctly and each one should have either a first name or two initials. (Not Mrs. E. Jones.)

Churches seldom make the most of picture possibilities. Some rural papers have no facilities for making engravings and it may be necessary for the churches to have the "cut" made at its own expense. Whether the paper or the church photographer takes the picture, however, great care should be taken in posing it. There is nothing duller than four persons lined up shoulder-to-shoulder as though they were facing a firing squad. Get some action into it, if possible. It is more interesting to see a person painting a poster or tacking it to a bulletin board than merely facing the camera holding the poster. If a new president is being installed, she should be shown receiving the gavel or a handshake from the out-going president. Instead of picturing a bazaar committee staring mutely into the camera, show the members making some eye-catching objects.

A little imagination can put life into a picture. Don't let your subjects just stand there!

Making Little Ones Out of Big Ones

One way to miss the chance for several stories is to cram too much material into one. This one, for instance, appeared one day in the paper:

> St. Paul's —— Church voted last night to undertake a fund drive for $200,000 to build a new education building on two acres of land on Lawson Street donated to the church by Mr. and Mrs. John R. Barker.
>
> Herbert Smith, chairman of the building fund campaign, announced that a solicitation of the membership will begin Feb. 9 following the publication of a brochure and other promotional materials providing information for potential contributors.
>
> Special gifts will be solicited for the auditorium to be known as Murray Memorial Hall in memory of Albert A. Murray who died last year after serving as a trustee of the church for thirty-seven years.
>
> The present church school quarters are inadequate to take care of the enrollment which has increased from 180 to 275 children in the last five years, Mr. Smith stated. The new building will contain twelve classrooms and staff offices in addition to the auditorium.
>
> Assisting Mr. Smith on the committee will be ——, . . .

Instead of one story there should have been at least six spread over several weeks.

Obviously, the first one should have pre-dated the building campaign announcement by at least a month: the gift of the land to the church. That should have been a major news item accompanied by a picture of Mr. Barker turning over the deed to the church. The story would have included a brief description of the site, uses to which it had previously been put, former owners, assessed valuation.

The first news "break" on the big story should concentrate on the announcement that the church has voted to construct a new $200,000 building on that site. Included would be a description of the conditions which make the new building necessary, general description of the proposed structure, background on previous improvement projects of the church, and the date of construction of the original building.

The second story should be on the fund-raising plans announcing the date and describing in detail the type of campaign to be conducted.

The chairman should have a story to himself leading with his appointment to the post and including a description of his business or professional background, other services he has performed for the church or community and a quotation from him on the need for the new building.

Other stories will also suggest themselves and at least four pictures: the chairman, an architect's rendering of the new building, a crowded classroom in the present quarters, a committee at work.

Making Big Ones Out of Little Ones

In addition to reporting the news which naturally occurs in a church, an imaginative publicity committee should seize every opportunity to create news. In this venture, every organization chairman should be eager to cooperate.

As an example of making news, let us imagine that Easter letters are about to be mailed to the congregation. Instead of taking care of it the routine way in the church office, the publicity committee can set up an "assembly line" of young people around a table—some folding, some filling the envelopes, some sealing and stamping, others serving refreshments. A picture can be taken either there or at the post office where two youngsters with their arms loaded with letters are inserting them in the mail slot.

It is difficult to imagine any meeting or project involving even a routine task which cannot be built up into an item with news value.

Getting Along With the Editor

Relations with editors and reporters vary greatly with the size of the community. On a large city paper, it is difficult to establish any kind of durable contact with the editors because there are so many of them. Many of the right hands do not know what the left hands are doing, and if you call in reference to a story you have turned in, you may never locate the man you gave it to.

In smaller communities, on the other hand, it is advisable to learn to know the editor and to feel that he knows you. You should make friendly contact also with the reporter who handles your material and, if a story is inaccurate or badly handled, he will appreciate it if you will settle the matter quietly and tactfully with him instead of going over his head to the boss.

Letters from a church should go to an editor at least

twice a year thanking him for the space devoted to church news and for the courteous cooperation of his staff. He likes to have a telephone call now and then saying a particular story was well-written. It is a tribute to a paper when reprints are made of a story for wide distribution to a congregation. (This is sometimes done to help promote a major fund-raising project or membership drive.)

We should recognize an editor's prestige in the community. Invite him and his wife to attend a church dinner once a year to be seated with guests of honor and introduced. During Newspaper Week he and members of his staff should be feted in some way. Ask him to speak at a church function or organization meeting. If there is an inter-church council in your community which occasionally invites the mayor or other prominent citizens to lunch, the newspaper editors should be included. To put it bluntly, we should cultivate their good will.

Even though we assume in general that editors judge a church story solely on its news value, there may be cases where an editor appears to be influenced by whim or prejudice and the question then is how to handle the situation. First of all, we might as well face the fact that no one ever wins an argument with a newspaper and no one ever advances his cause by antagonizing an editor or going over his head no matter how justified we feel our complaint to be. In most cases a steady flow of well-prepared news stories submitted without complaints, will eventually find its way through personal barriers. If a case proves particularly difficult, we should try to discover why. Sometimes a resentment dates back many years to a time when the church vigorously opposed a stand the paper took politically or socially. A deep-rooted antagonism may go back to personal friction with a minister or layman. In these cases, if a minister and one or two laymen with a pleasant and diplomatic approach will sit down and talk the problem over with an editor, there is a good chance that the situation can be resolved.

It is important to assume, however, that his judgment as a newspaperman is sound even though it might not coincide with our desires as church workers.

How to Do It

When you ask your editor whether he wants you to write your stories or submit a list of facts to be turned over to a reporter, he will probably defer his answer until he sees what kind of news copy you write.

A sure way to establish a pleasant reputation in a newspaper office is to submit material which is accurate, thorough, concise, and expertly written in the style of the paper. The way to become familiar with the style is to read the paper studiously. Many papers will give you a "style book" listing their preferences in the use of abbreviations, titles, punctuation, capitalization, and other variables. One thing cannot be said too emphatically or too often: GET YOUR MATERIAL TO THE PAPER AS FAR IN ADVANCE OF THE DEADLINE AS POSSIBLE! Be as conscientious about covering an event for the paper as you were to have your advance stories printed.

The most important part of a news story just as in your parish paper is the lead—or opening paragraph. With that, you either win or lose your reader. If you want him to stay with you, the lead had better catch his eye and hold his attention. Never describe a meeting chronologically. You are not writing minutes. You are writing something you want somebody to read so you therefore confront him with the most important thing you have to say—first. Give him as much as you can in the first paragraph because he may not have time to read any further.

Learn to put yourself in the reader's place. What would hold *you?*

"The regular monthly meeting of the vestry . . ."? No. "A talk on missions was given last night by . . ."? No. "James A. Johnson, executive secretary of the Promotion and Cultivation Department of the Division of World Missions of the Manhattan Branch of the . . ."? Oh—No!

If the program you are covering featured a speaker, lead off either with a condensed version of his conclusion or the most salient point he made:

"The lag in church support of missions is opening the door to communism in India, David P. Conroy declared last night at a meeting of the Men's Club at the First Presbyterian Church."

If an election was the main business of the meeting, lead with that. Not "Officers were elected . . . ," but "Mrs. Samuel Curry was elected president of the Business Women's Club last night at the annual meeting in the parish house. She succeeds. . . ."

If there was no speaker and no election, perhaps some action was taken.

"A gift of $100 to the building fund of the First Baptist Church was voted last night by the Men's Club at a meeting in the parish house."

If there was no speaker, no election and no action taken, the last resort is, "Thirty persons attended a meeting of. . . ."

A daily perusal of leads in the major metropolitan dailies is a fruitful experience. Not only will you learn the characteristics of a good one—you will also notice a wide range of quality. Even in a top-flight paper, leads are not always uniformly good.

Here are the ways in which two writers handled the same story in two New York City papers:

> "President Eisenhower took a hopeful view of the world today and the chances of keeping the peace."
>
> "President Eisenhower today rejected emphatically the idea of preventive war and instead saw the free world entering a new era of opportunity to build a strong and enduring peace."

Notice those words, "rejected emphatically."

Here are three leads on the same story from Marblehead, Mass., by the Associated Press, the United Press, and a Special to the New York *Times* (not in the order listed).

1. "A member of the Marblehead Race Week Committee said 'seventy-five to eighty' sailboats capsized off this port in a violent thunder squall today, but no casualties were reported."
2. "A brief, violent thunder squall overturned sixty-one sailing craft during a series of races in Marblehead harbor today, but tragedy was averted through quick work by power boat operators in the area."
3. "Nearly 100 sailboats capsized in Marblehead harbor today when a sudden thunder squall swept across the water in the middle of a sailing race."

Notice the first nine words of each lead. Don't follow the wrong example!

PART III

The Church Budget

PART III
is dedicated to the Rev. Asbury G. E. Stromberg, pastor of the Mamaroneck Methodist Church from 1941 to 1951, who knew it could be done.

Chapter V

Pumping Life Into Your Budget

On a winter evening in 1945, ten members of a finance committee sat in the parish house of a 700-member church in a suburban community.

There was no way out of it. The budget would be over $8,500 for the coming year.

One member repeated a remark he had made twice before: "I still say wait until we see how much money we get—and then decide what we can do."

A succession of comments followed.

"The roof certainly won't wait another year."

"Yes, but there's a limit to what you can get out of these people. We've had enough trouble making our *old* budget."

"Money's getting tighter all the time."

"Suppose we draw up an 'absolute minimum' budget—and then list a few of these other items at the bottom? If we get the money—all right, we'll take care of them."

This happened to be the first meeting for one of the members; he had come from a wide-awake church where finances had posed no problem. In his new church, he had offered to serve on the finance committee, but he was obviously baffled by the procedure at this meeting.

"How do you raise money here, anyway?" he asked.

"No one has ever called on our family to ask for a pledge."

It was explained that on Loyalty Sunday, pledge cards were placed in the pews. After a talk on the church's needs by the chairman of the finance committee and a sermon by the minister on stewardship, members filled in the cards and put them in the collection plates. Loyalty Day was preceded by a letter to the members urging their support and enclosing a copy of the budget. The week following Loyalty Day, another letter with a pledge card was sent to all members who had not been in church. After two weeks had elapsed, callers went out to collect the cards which had not been mailed in.

"Don't you ever have an every-member canvass?" the new man asked.

"We tried that," was the reply. "But it's hard to get people to go out and ask for money. They just won't do it."

The new member glanced around the room. "There are ten of us here," he said. "If we could each get five other men, we'd have sixty callers, and we could do the whole job in one afternoon."

The committee looked at him numbly.

"Five men?" one of them finally murmured. "I couldn't get five men. I couldn't find five men who would do it. You just can't get people to go out and ask for money."

The discussion continued for another hour, and when the meeting ended, the budget had been increased by about ten per cent and the new member of the committee had agreed to serve as chairman of the budget campaign.

On Budget Sunday, seventy-two workers went out calling and in two hours, the new budget was over-subscribed.

That day marked the start of a new era for that church.

It was the beginning of the education of a parish. In ten years the budget was quadrupled—without any major net increase in membership. The somber, fearful attitude of the finance committee had undergone a complete transformation. From "wait and see how much money we get," the philosophy had changed to "let's decide what this church should be doing in this community, and then we'll get whatever money is needed"!

The church "breathes" with freedom now. It has a constant margin for progress. No longer constricted by financial worries, it is vigorous, fearless, and propelled by creative faith.

How was this transformation accomplished?

In two ways: this church changed its attitude toward money; and it changed its method of raising it.

1. CHANGING THE ATTITUDE

Before 1943, the church had allowed itself to feel apologetic about asking for money. The committee seemed to feel guilty of unwarranted extravagance when the budget was increased. Sensitive to the charge that "the church is always asking for money," the committee tried to keep financial matters as quiet as possible. It tried to be "realistic." That word has become as overworked a cliché as you'll find anywhere in the English language. Lack of vision, penury, fear, and pessimism can usually be found lurking behind it. The word "realistic" is definable only in terms of the faith of the person who uses it. One man says, "We must be realistic"—and keeps the budget at the same figure. Another man says, "All right, let's BE realistic" and he doubles the budget. He sees to it that the budget is underwritten, too!

One of the first things Mr. New Member did was to take the apology out of fund raising. The church is always needing more money? Of course it is! Is it a strain on the spiritual life of the church to acknowledge that soap powder and electricity and hymn books have to be paid for? So is your school district always asking for money—and your fuel company and your grocer. Or perhaps you pay *them* before they ask.

Right here, incidentally, is where your complainant condemns himself. If the church must ask constantly for money, whose fault is it? It's like the old chestnut about the man who said his wife was always asking him for money. "She asked me for ten dollars two weeks ago, ten dollars last week, five dollars this week," he complained.

"What does she do with all that money?" his friend asked.

"I don't know," was the reply. "I haven't given her any yet."

Mr. New Member accomplished one important thing that first year. He made it clear through the publicity which was sent out and in talks to workers that, although the church is primarily an institution with a spiritual function, it is also an administrative unit with a plant to be maintained, salaries to be paid, and a program to be supported.

The finance committee began to feel that perhaps the job it was doing had the mark of respectability after all.

A second attitude which had to be changed was the "small change" feeling with which most contributors approached their church envelopes.

There were too many twenty, twenty-five, thirty-five cent pledges. They had stayed at that level for years. It was clear that church-giving was regarded on a small change level—clearly a holdover from Sunday school days.

Again through graphic leaflets and brief messages on postal cards, Mr. New Member suggested that most members were putting the church in the same category as a tip to a waiter.

One of the publicity leaflets asked frankly what a businessman's luncheon tips amounted to in the course of a week. Then the potent question was put: "ARE YOU REALLY *SUPPORTING* YOUR CHURCH—or are you just tipping it?"

Publicity directed toward children stressed twenty-five cents as an amount which could be given to the church just by sacrificing one ice cream soda each week. As twenty-five cents began to be identified with a child's gift, the adult pledges began to climb.

Brief messages were designed for persons in various categories of giving. To the thirty-five-centers, it was pointed out that if twenty such pledges could be increased to fifty cents for the coming year, the church would have $156 more and could buy new chairs for a Sunday school room. If ten persons giving $1.50 could raise their pledges to $2.00, the church would have $260 more and could repair the furnace.

The specific appeal which related definite sums to definite needs brought results and the pledges climbed still higher.

Special attention was given to members who were reluctant to sign pledge cards. First of all it was stressed that a pledge indicates only what the signer hopes to be able to do and is in no way binding if he finds he is unable to pay. But great emphasis was placed on the necessity of knowing ahead of time what the church can expect to receive. One communication to the non-pledgers enclosed a small white envelope. The letter asked, "How would you feel if your pay envelope contained this?" In the small envelope was a question mark. It was pointed out that the recipient would not know how to plan the support of his family or the maintenance of his home for the coming year if he was in doubt about his income.

The number of pledges climbed from 300 in 1945, to 348 in 1946, to 385 in 1947. The increase has been steady ever since.

There was some agitation at first over the question of sending out quarterly statements.

"That's a sure way to make people mad," one of the committee members claimed.

Convinced that a reaction is determined not by what you do but how you do it, the committee voted to send statements worded like this:

"We are frequently asked by members for information regarding the status of their church pledges. Others tell us they anticipate our quarterly communications before bringing their giving up to date. Believing, therefore, that contributors are always glad to know how their accounts stand, we furnish the following information: . . . ."

No one has testified yet to being "mad." On the contrary, the gesture was interpreted as a business-like way of conducting the church's financial affairs. The amount of uncollected pledges at the end of a year has dropped from around fourteen per cent to between seven and eight per cent.

As the years passed, the bulk of the pledges rose from the thirty-five and fifty-cent level to the one-, two-, and three-dollar level. The parishioners have been made aware of the fact, through well-directed publicity, that the church depends upon them for *support;* that it has no money but theirs.

2. CHANGING THE METHOD

If you are wondering how Mr. New Member got seventy-two workers and oversubscribed the budget that first year, this is how it was accomplished.

The first thing he did was to sit down with the minister and the finance committee chairman and scan the church's membership list. They chose about thirty persons to serve on a general campaign committee, some to handle publicity, some to serve as captains of calling teams, some to plan a workers' luncheon, some to organize the membership geographically and compile callers' lists.

The second job was to recruit the workers. It was obvious that the man who had claimed he did not know five persons who would go calling was thinking in terms of the same old faithfuls who had been breaking their backs in various church jobs for years.

A list was made of every man on the church mailing list; not just members—but *every man*. It included fathers of Sunday school children, husbands who came to church only on Easter, "friends" who attended social events but seldom showed up at services—everyone who was even remotely related to any phase of the church program.

The list contained 260 names!

The following communication was sent to every man on the list:

HELP WANTED: MEN! (60 of them)

Whether you go to church once a year, now and then, or every Sunday; whether you belong to this church or no church has nothing to do with this letter.

We need your help in a special way on April 15th and we believe there are enough men interested in seeing the church run on a business-like basis to devote 90 minutes to putting it there!

By the time April 15th arrives, every member and friend of the church will know that a campaign is under way in high gear. The Promotion Committee will have informed every constituent of all the details of the drive and, by April 15th, he will know what part he will be able to play in it. On that day, we want ten teams of six men each to call for the signed pledges and we believe, by concerted effort, we can add a MARGIN FOR PROGRESS to our present budget and program.

This is the way it will work:

On April 2nd, Mr. A. will receive a letter explaining the campaign and what the church hopes to accomplish through an expanded program.

On April 6th, he will receive an illustrated card urging him to join the Margin for Progress by either increasing his pledge or making one for the first time.

On April 10th, Mr. A. will receive a letter explaining what the church will be able to do if he increases his pledge.

On April 12th, he will receive an illustrated booklet showing what the present program is and what it could be with a MARGIN FOR PROGRESS.

On April 14th, he will receive a card saying, "Tomorrow at 3:30 P. M., Mr. .... will call on you to receive your pledge."

The day of the drive, April 15th, a buffet luncheon will be served at 1 P. M. and, with 60 men ready to start, not more than six cards will be assigned to each man. The full job should be done within an hour and a half.

Maybe you've never done any kind of work for the church before. On the other hand, maybe you help in many ways in many departments. In either case, we need you now in this special way.

When one of the team lieutenants calls you, let him know you will be willing to give those minutes of effort to establish for the church a MARGIN FOR PROGRESS.

Sincerely,

Chairman

The finance committee was reconvened and Mr. New Member took the scissors and cut the list of 260 names in ten parts. Each man was given a section containing twenty-six names. Out of the twenty-six, did anyone think he couldn't get *five?*

There was no one who did not get five. In fact, those who called the entire list had seven, eight, and nine. The difficulty was that several stopped their telephoning after they got the required number and the church office received calls from men who had received the letter but had not been called! In subsequent years, everybody on each list was called and so many workers were obtained that the finance committee lieutenants were relieved of the job of canvassing and were free to supervise their workers and follow up uncompleted calls.

A great deal of study was given to the recruiting of the callers. It was obvious that these men could not be expected "to go out and ask for money." Many of them had never taken an interest in the church and knew very little about it. A man who himself did not support the church could not be expected to solicit a pledge from some active member who had supported it for years. Many were diffident about ringing a doorbell and others were at a loss to know how to discuss church support.

They were assured, therefore, that the task of explanation and promotion would be done for them ahead of time by publicity sent through the mail. The parishioner would be expecting the call and would be prepared. The caller was provided with postal cards to be sent out the Thursday before the drive, informing the recipient that at 3:30 P.M. on Sunday, Mr. So-and-So would call to obtain his pledge to the church for the coming year.

One man remarked frankly, "I don't know what to say when the person opens the door."

To make it as easy as possible for those whose problems were as elementary as that, the committee devised a gimmick which developed into a major factor in obtaining new and increased pledges. Three pledge cards were printed in different colors. One was a blue card with the words, "Increased Pledge," printed at the top. Another was pink and contained the words, "New Pledge." The third was a white card for pledges which would be the same as the preceding year.

Anybody can say, "Which color card would you like to sign?"

When the pledger asks, "What's the difference?" the caller explains—and perhaps adds, "We hope you will want to sign the pink card since our budget is larger for next year."

Not only does that device make the conversation easier, it also facilitates the bookkeeping because the increased and new pledges can be quickly spotted as the cards are collected at the close of the afternoon.

The workers attended church in a group on Budget Sunday and at the close of the service were guests at a luncheon provided by one of the guilds. Materials were distributed, the workers were dedicated to their task by the minister, the chairman delivered a brief and inspiring pep talk, and the teams were dispatched to return in an hour and a half with the job done.

The report room had the semblance of election night as the men returned. They waited in excited clusters as the cards were tabulated. They peered over the shoulders of the man at the adding machine. When it became clear that the goal was in sight—and finally that it had been reached and passed, a spontaneous cheer peppered with hand clapping filled the room.

The spirit generated by the success of that day's work permeated the entire parish and laid a solid foundation for the success of budget drives in years to come. Perhaps the most significant result of all was that many men who had had no previous interest in the church began to appear at the worship services and it soon became evident that they, too, were becoming educated to the necessity of supporting their church with their prayers, their presence, and their gifts.

In succeeding years, these men have gradually learned how to talk about the church. Although the major job of education and promotion is still done by the publicity committee through advance leaflets and brochures, the callers have learned the technique of "selling" an expanding budget which makes their job far pleasanter than it was ten years ago.

The publicity has veered as far as possible from traditional letter-writing. Communications are designed to be read at a glance.

The cover of a leaflet always contains a few words which impel the reader to open it and look inside: "Without You," "State Aid for the Church?," "It's Time to Ask Four Questions," "It's Too Late," "Are You The Man Who Says, 'The Church Is Always Asking For Money?,' " "When Should A Church Stop Growing?"

In the corner of every envelope, a message is printed which distinguishes it from other church letters: "15 PER CENT MORE," "MARGIN FOR PROGRESS," "COMING APRIL 12th."

Here are three messages sent to prospective workers:

WELL, MEN, IT'S YOUR TIME OF THE YEAR!

The annual church finance campaign has become such a habitual procedure that we know all you are waiting for is a notice of the date and the time.

So—here it is. The date is APRIL 11th.

The dinner will be served by the Service Guild in the Church Parlors at 12:30 P.M.

REMEMBER—it's a one-day drive. The promotion is done for you by mail ahead of time. If every man does his part, no one will have to make more than six calls. Unless you stop to visit at too many firesides, you should be all through and back at your gardening in two hours!

REMEMBER—there are 8,784 hours in the year (leap year) and your church asks for only two of them to put our finance drive over the top.

REMEMBER—one of the lieutenants will telephone you before March 19 to enlist your help on his team. You will send out postal cards to the names on your list telling them what time you will call to pick up their pledge cards.

REMEMBER—April 11th———two hours———$18,000.

GABRIEL WENDEL,
Chairman

MEN...

YOUR TWO HOURS ARE COMING UP!

IN 1945 ● WE EMBARKED ON A NEW PROJECT!
We set a budget goal and then appealed to you to put the job over. You succeeded with flying colors!

IN 1946 ● AGAIN, WE SOLD YOU A BILL OF GOODS!
You responded with gusto and in one afternoon the budget was underwritten.

IN 1947 ● THE CHURCH FINANCIAL DRIVE
has definitely become a man's job. You rolled up your sleeves and again, we reached the goal!

IN 1948 ● WE NO LONGER HAD TO SELL THE IDEA.
Men who never did any other church work were awaiting our call.

IN 1949 ● IT HAD BECOME A HABIT!
Two hours a year for the church budget! All you wanted to know was the date and time.

WE'LL MAKE IT BRIEF!
We're counting on you to help.

THIS YEAR

THE DATE • APRIL 16th

THE TIME • 11:00 A.M. CHURCH SERVICE
12:30 P.M. LUNCHEON IN THE CHURCH PARLOR
1:30 P. M. CANVAS STARTS!

THE GOAL • $22,500

A LIEUTENANT WILL CALL YOU SOON, TO INVITE YOU TO SERVE ON HIS TEAM!

May 13th is Mothers' Day
June 14th is Flag Day
June 17th is Fathers' Day
March 25th is Easter Day
Monday is Wash Day
Oct. 12th is Columbus Day
Nov. 6th is Election Day
Sept. 3rd is Labor Day
June 10th is Children's Day
July 4th is Independence Day

AND, MEN,

APRIL 22nd IS YOUR DAY

YOUR DAY TO GIVE 2 HOURS TO YOUR CHURCH

YOUR DAY TO CALL ON SIX PERSONS

YOUR DAY TO HELP UNDERWRITE THE BUDGET

11 A.M. Church Service
12:30 P.M. Luncheon
1:30 P.M. Canvass starts
3:30 P.M. All through

A lieutenant will call you soon to enlist your help.

Saturday is Pay Day
Feb. 14th is Valentine's Day
Dec. 25th is Christmas Day
Nov. 11th is Armistice Day
Jan. 1st is New Year's Day
March 17th is St. Patrick's Day
Feb. 2nd was St. Swithin's Day
Nov. 22nd is Thanksgiving Day
June 11th is Kamehameha Day
May 30th is Memorial Day

The first step toward training was taken the second year, when the following skit was presented at the luncheon:

MR. JONES LEARNS HOW

by Dorothy and Carl Allensworth

NARRATOR

In approaching people for money for the Church, there are certain "do's" and "don'ts." In order to bring some of these to your attention, I've asked Mr. Durable Jones to re-enact his own experience. (*Enter Jones, with a handful of cards, pamphlets, etc., tries to sort them as* NARRATOR *continues. Mr. Jones' hat is on the back of his head, tie is askew, coat unbuttoned.*) Now, when Mr. Jones started, some four years ago, he was a little green.

JONES

(*Knocks on door, fumbles with cards. Door opened by man. Jones, startled, drops cards, bends over to pick a few up.*) How do you do Mr.—ah—Smith, no—I mean Mr. Brown, no—I mean—ah—

MAN

Martin.

JONES

Oh, yes, Mr. Martin. I have your card here some where. (*Fumbles for it.*)

MARTIN

Well?

JONES

I don't suppose you'd like to give some money to the Church, would you?

MARTIN

No, I wouldn't. (*Slams door.*)

JONES

(*Continues to pick up cards and sort them as* NARRATOR *continues.*)

NARRATOR

Needless to say, Mr. Jones was not very successful at raising money that year. But Jones was a stubborn character. His second year he was determined to improve:

JONES

(*Strides briskly up to same door, knocks. Door opened by second man.*) How do you do, Mr. King. I'm Mr. Jones. May I have a few minutes of your time?

KING

Well, I don't know. What do you want with it?

JONES

I want to ask you to pledge some money to the Church.

KING

Pledge? I put money in the plate every Sunday.

JONES

I know. But the Church needs more money.

KING

So do I, brother. I've got one daughter in college, the other daughter getting married next month, and my wife says we need a new car. I just don't see how we can afford to give anything more to the Church. Maybe next year things will be different. Come and see me then. Good-by. (*Shuts door.*)

JONES

Well—ah—. (*Door shuts.*) Good-by.

NARRATOR

(*Jones scratches his head, puts hat on straight, straightens his tie, buttons his coat, while* NARRATOR *speaks.*) Poor Mr. Jones. He knew what he wanted to say, but he just wasn't able to get it out in time. But Jones is not a man who gives up easily, and he did learn from his experiences. When he went out the third year, he had high hopes.

JONES

(*Knocks on same door. Door opens on third man. Jones attacks with great enthusiasm.*) Good afternoon, Mr. McKinley. I'd like to tell you something about the work of our Church. Did you know that the Church houses and provides for more than twenty-three community activities, such as choirs, Boy Scouts, Cub Scouts, Camp Fire Girls, youth groups, boys' groups, girls' groups, women's groups, men's groups, and concerts?

MCKINLEY

No. I didn't know.

JONES

(*With more fire, and all in one breath, counting items off on fingers.*) Did you know that the Church aids charitable groups all over the world, including summer camps, boys' camps, girls' camps, underprivileged children, foreign hospitals, foreign orphanages, local hospitals and local schools?

MCKINLEY

You don't say.

JONES

(*A little taken back.*) Don't you think these things are tremendously important?

MCKINLEY

Well, I guess so. But why are you telling me all this?

JONES

Mr. McKinley, I've come to ask you to increase your pledge to the Church this year. In order to carry on all these activities, the Church is badly in need of extra funds.

MCKINLEY

Well, perhaps I can increase it a little.

JONES

(*Excited.*) Fine. Fine. I'm delighted to hear you say that. You know, the dollar isn't worth as much as it used to be.

MCKINLEY

It sure isn't.

JONES

Why, I can remember when you used to be able to buy a pound of steak for fifty-nine cents; you could get a good suit of clothes for forty dollars. But today! Why the cost of food and clothing and everything is just terrible.

MCKINLEY

That's right, I hadn't thought about that. Come to think of it, I don't believe I can afford to increase my pledge this year. I'm still making the same as I made last year, and I'm having to pay more for everything I buy. You better put me down for the same amount that I gave last year.

JONES

But you said. . . .

MCKINLEY

Sorry, but you know how it is. Good-by, Mr. Jones, nice talking to you. (*Shuts door.*)

JONES

(*To no one.*) Good-by. (*Jones takes off hat, slams it on floor, looks at it, picks it up again, puts on head, straightens clothes and gets ready to try the next year, while* NARRATOR *speaks.*)

NARRATOR

Well, he almost made it that time. At least, he got his story out. In fact, he got a little too much of his story out. Mr. Jones didn't know when to quit. But he was still willing to try it again the next year:

JONES

(*Knocks on door. Door opened by fourth man.*) How do you do, Mr. Howe. I'm Mr. Jones from our Church.

HOWE

Oh yes, Mr. Jones. Glad to see you.

JONES

I hope your wife is feeling better, I heard she was ill.

HOWE

Yes, she was—the grippe—but she's much better now.

JONES

Fine. I've come to talk to you about your generous support of the work of our Church. I don't have to tell you how important that work is. I'm sure you know as well as I do what it means to the community, to the nation, and to the world.

HOWE

Yes, I have a pretty good idea.

JONES

And I'm sure you'll agree that the work should not be curtailed, if anything it should be extended. But the difficulty is that the Church's costs have increased just like all other costs, so that we can't do as many things for the same amount of money this year as we could last year.

HOWE

Yes, I'm aware of that.

JONES

So, what we're asking is that each member raise his pledge a little to allow us to be of at least as much service as we were last year.

HOWE

Well, of course, I'm in the same predicament. My money won't buy as much as it did last year, either.

JONES

That's quite true. I suppose it's really a matter of what seems more important. Now, twenty-five cents more a week, or thirteen dollars a year, would mean a small sacrifice to you, but it might save an underprivileged child in Europe or Asia from starvation.

HOWE

Well, when you put it that way, it does seem as though most everyone could give up that much.

JONES

Mr. Howe, may I put you down for $13.00 a year in addition to your regular pledge? (*Has card out, with pencil to mark on it.*)

HOWE

Yes, I guess that's agreeable.

JONES

Thank you. It's been a real pleasure to talk to you Mr. Howe. Glad Mrs. Howe feels better. Good-by.

HOWE

Good-by, Mr. Jones. (*Shuts door.*)
(*Jones takes out handkerchief, mops brow.*)

NARRATOR

So, Durable Jones finally won his letter, and I've no doubt that all of you will do the same.

Ready-made materials for promoting a budget drive and for facilitating the work of the callers is available from the headquarters of most denominations and also from interdenominational agencies. Participation in the United Church Canvass in November insures a committee not only valuable working materials but also the benefit of community-wide publicity.

The small turn-over charts which can be placed on a living room table are helpful tools in the graphic explanation of a church's financial needs. With the help of a local artist, fifteen or so pages can be prepared illustrating various categories of the budget and reproduced by photo offset to provide a copy for each team of callers.

It has been found that here and there a discontented parishioner seizes the occasion to register complaints about the church and its ministry.

These comments are always listed and referred to the public relations committee for careful study. A conscientious effort is made to straighten out any difficulty which the worker has detected. Workers are provided with suggestions for handling these situations.

In many cases the workers have assumed a public relations function and have left disgruntled persons far happier than they found them. They also return with up-to-date facts for the church records and valuable information which the minister should have.

There is an inevitable question asked on the subject of recruiting canvassers. "You keep talking about teams of *men*. Don't women make as good callers as men?"

For a general parish visitation, certainly. But when it comes to a finance drive, there is a strong argument in favor of men. There is no doubt that in every church there are women who are fitted for such a task—but we cannot escape the fact that in the eyes of most men, a woman's devotion to her church is expressed through the guilds and other societies, the church school, and in the pews. There is no doubt, either, that a woman could make an excellent usher. But for some unexplainable reason, it is more fitting for a man to do it. It somehow seems more impressive for a business man to sit down with another business or professional man to discuss the business of the church. It is no reflection upon the women. This is a woman talking!

In March, 1956, the finance committee met again in the same room. Last year the budget was raised $5,000 to an unprecedented total of $33,100. This year there were crucial maintenance needs, increases in salaries, an enlarged view of benevolences, a mortgage to be paid off.

Our man, no longer a new member after eleven years, looked around the room as his colleagues were busy with their pencils. Six of the members were veterans of that first committee. Six others had been added in succeeding years. The figures were totaled and the chairman announced, "It looks like $37,655 for next year." There were no adverse or pessimistic remarks—but what was even more significant, there was no hopeful or optimistic comment either! The committee had come to the place where the success of the drive was a foregone conclusion. Success was taken for granted.

Before we leave this story of a church which has allowed itself to grow, the most important thing of all must be said.

The minister and leaders who brought about this change in attitude and method were impelled by one indispensable ingredient: *the faith that it could be done*. By "faith" we do not mean mere optimism or hope. We mean complete and utter conviction. As each year's budget was totaled and each goal announced, its achievement was already a fact.

When a ferryboat approaches a slip, a rope is tossed around a stake. That means the destination of the boat has been irrevocably determined. All that is then necessary is the exertion of sufficient muscular or mechanical energy to bring the craft in.

Something like that happens when the confident mind reaches out and "lassoes" a target. Without that creative faith, all the energy in the world will not bring the boat home. With it, success is inevitable.

Chapter VI

Want a Fifteen Per Cent Increase?

Ask a friend why he gives money to the church.

He'll probably give you some nebulous answer like, "That's part of being a church member" or "Everybody has to help out."

Actually, when everything has been said on the subject of personal responsibility and Christian stewardship, one incontrovertible fact remains: a person gives to his church because he knows it needs money to operate. The size of his gift depends upon the extent of his knowledge of the specific need. A person with a vague feeling of responsibility might pledge $100 for the year. But go to him and say, "You tripped on the sidewalk tonight because there is no light out there. Will you contribute ten dollars toward the cost of installing one?" And the chances are he will write you a check without hesitation.

The finance committee of the church we have been describing decided two years ago that a successful budget campaign should be based on two simple facts: a person will give if he knows exactly what the money will be used for; a person will increase his previous year's giving if he has a graphic picture of the increased need.

It was decided that a promotional program based on those two convictions could easily result in a fifteen per cent increase in the budget. This chapter will describe in detail how it was done.

The committee voted first of all to present the budget needs at a congregational dinner.

That decision was not made easily. Would people come to a dinner when they knew you were going to talk about money? Was it fair to ask the women to cook one more meal when they had already provided several during the year for other purposes? Could you get enough people to pitch in and help with such a program? It was nearing the end of the season and everybody was tired.

The committee was finally convinced that people could be lured to the dinner if they knew it would be a pleasant, entertaining affair; also that the meal could be planned so that none of the old-timers would have to work at all.

The next question was—should the dinner be free or should they sell tickets? After all, they asked, would people *pay* to come to church to sign a pledge card? Others argued that unless tickets were sold, there would be no way of knowing how many to expect and bad weather might cut down the attendance. It was decided that tickets would be sold for one dollar, that an ample meal would be served, and the deficit made up from the promotion fund in the budget.

1. GETTING THE PEOPLE THERE

There are at least seven ways of getting people out to a church function.

a. Assure them that they will enjoy themselves.
b. Give them a job to do in connection with the event.
c. Work their children into the program.
d. Show pictures in which they know they will appear.
e. Convince them through attractive publicity that it is a major event in the life of the church.
f. Telephone them.
g. Make arrangements for the care of their children.

All these methods were employed and it was still not an easy matter to convince them that a finance dinner could be fun. By working assiduously, however, the committee turned out 200 persons to the dinner—a capacity crowd for the dining room.

2. THE MENU

With the dual purpose of giving the veteran cooks a rest and recruiting as many workers as possible, it was decided that most of the food should be prepared at home and brought to the kitchen ready to serve. With that in mind, the following menu was devised: tomato juice, baked ham, whipped Idaho potatoes, frozen peas, fruit jello salad, rolls, ginger bread with whipped cream, coffee.

For each item on the menu, a committee was appointed and the membership list was divided for calling purposes. Twenty persons were each asked to bring a pan of salad which could be divided into nine portions. Twenty were asked to bake a pan of prepared ginger bread. Twenty were asked to bring five potatoes each—the halves whipped and refilled ready for browning in the church ovens. Others were asked to bring cans of chilled tomato juice, mayonnaise, lettuce cleaned and ready to serve, cans of coffee. A parishioner who had "connections" with a food company managed to get frozen peas donated. A local milk company made a sizeable contribution of cream. A bakery gave the rolls. The committee purchased only the hams, sugar, and butter.

Much to the committee's surprise, instead of having to make up a deficit from the treasury, they realized a profit of $100 on the dinner. Best of all, women were seen passing through the kitchen who had never been in it before!

3. RECRUITING THE WORKERS

Anyone who has ever worked on a church dinner knows that that meal could have been cooked and served by half a dozen women. But the effort to interest as many persons as possible resulted in the participation of 131 persons—many of them new members.

Committees were improvised for the sole purpose of giving new people jobs. In addition to the menu committees, the following groups were organized:

Invitation committee to prepare and mail invitations to the entire constituency.

Ticket committee for printing and distributing tickets.
Dining room committee for the setting of tables.
Decoration committee.
Waiters.
Art committee to make place cards for the speakers' table and kits from multi-colored "construction" paper for each place. (These were folded and the pockets stapled. They contained a pledge card, pencil, a mimeographed copy of the program and leaflets describing missionary projects of the church-at-large.)
Publicity committee.
Sitters (High school girls who "sat" with small children at home. A supper was served for twenty-five cents in another part of the church for older children followed by movies.)
Telephone committee.
Clean-up committee.
Program committee (Four large groups).

The following incident will show to what ends the planners went to put people to work. When all the jobs had been assigned, there were six willing women who had nothing to do. They or their husbands were important "potentials" as pledge signers—so it was finally decided that the invitations should be hand addressed and these women went to work one afternoon in the church office writing names and addresses on envelopes.

Altogether, 209 persons had some job to do in connection with Easter Monday Fund-Day.

4. PUBLICITY

The publicity had two emphases. It aimed to get as many persons as possible out to the dinner and it hammered at the fact that the budget was to be increased fifteen per cent.

There were three channels: direct mail to the members, promotion in the church bulletin and parish paper, and stories in the local newspaper.

Two communications were sent through the mail. The first was a postal card three weeks before the dinner announcing the date, playing up the name "Easter Monday Fund-Day," and mentioning the fifteen per cent increase. The second was a folded leaflet. On the cover at zig-zag angles were the words: "Ever Hear A Budget Talk?," "Ever Watch a Budget Act?," "Ever Feel A Budget Come To Life?," "Ever See Where The Money Goes?"

The two inside pages contained "matchstick" sketches pertaining to the budget and a few lines in attractive type urging the reader to make reservations at once for the delicious Easter Monday Fund-Day dinner. On the back page the current and new budgets were printed making it clear that there was a fifteen per cent increase.

The parish paper announced the adoption of the new budget, stressed the total as compared with the current year and described the plans for Monday Fund-Day in detail, listing all committee members.

The stories in the newspaper carried the following headlines in the order in which they appeared:

CHURCH ADOPTS BUDGET OF $27,600
CHURCH'S BUILDING CHAIRMAN REPORTS
WENDEL TO HEAD CHURCH'S DRIVE
NINE NAMED TO CHURCH CANVASS POST
CHURCH TO DRAMATIZE "WALKING-TALKING" BUDGET
SLIDE PROGRAM TO BE SHOWN AT "EASTER MONDAY FUND-DAY"
CHURCH'S FINANCIAL PROGRAM DRAMATIZED AT DINNER EVENT

It should be stressed that, although the publicity undoubtedly made the people aware of the plans, it was the telephoning and the personal contacts which actually sold the tickets and brought the people to the dinner. Publicity alone should not be depended upon to bring out a crowd to any church event.

5. THE PROGRAM

The program, of course, was the most important part of the evening, the *raison d'etre* which really turned the trick. It will be outlined in detail and the scripts reproduced so that any church can adapt them to its own needs. The aim, remember, was two-fold. It was intended to show the people how the money was spent and to convince them that fifteen per cent more was needed for the coming year.

The budget items were divided into four parts: first, the "connectional" expenses due to the denomination at large, staff salaries, maintenance costs, and benevolences; second, housekeeping and utility expenses; third, minor items; fourth, local benevolences and World Service giving.

"Connectional," Salaries, Maintenance, Benevolence Expenses

These items were presented with the use of forty-six color slides. Many of them had been taken by the pastor through the year. Others were posed for this particular purpose. They are listed here and may be matched to the numbers in the script.

1. The church
2. The administrative head of the church-at-large
3. Regional administrator
4. Retired minister
5. Widow receiving check
6. Young minister receiving check
7. Church tower
8. Pastor in pulpit
9. Wedding
10. Baptisms
11. Pastor advising organization
12. Pastor counseling with parishioner
13. Youth worker with senior group
14. Youth worker with intermediates
15. Secretary at typewriter
16. Custodian ringing bell
17. Organist
18. Choir director with singer
19. Church

20. Parsonage
21. Parish House
22. Church official body
23. Church exterior being painted
24. Custodian spreading ashes
25. Custodian's helper mowing lawn
26. Outdoor fair
27. Flower garden
28. Church or tower
29. Senior choir
30. Junior choir
31. Group making choir robes
32. Beginner Department group
33. Nursery group
34. Recreation activity
35. Basketball game
36. Woman's group
37. Work group having snack
38. Camp Fire Girls
39. Girl Scouts
40. Boy or Cub Scouts
41. Small rural church
42. Orphans at Casa Materna
43. Naples slums
44. Casa Materna orphanage
45. Church
46. Narrator

And here is the script used with the slides. It should be remembered that it was written for a specific church. For the words "bishop" and "district superintendent," the administrators' titles in other denominations may of course be substituted.

(Slide 1) This is the story of OUR CHURCH

Let us ask ourselves for a moment—WHAT IS A CHURCH? Is it a building? Is it a congregation? Is it an institution? Is it a spiritual ideal?

It is all of these things, of course. We see here our beautiful building. It has been a spiritual beacon in this village for nearly one hundred years.

But think for a moment what our building would look like if there were no people worshiping in it . . . if there were no devotion, no faithful care. We all know what happens to an empty building. It soon becomes a blot on the landscape.

That will never happen to our church because of the people. Because of the thought and planning which is behind it every day of the year.

(2) Who is the person back of every church in the New York Area? Here is our Bishop in his office in New York. You will not find his name in our budget, but there is an item called "episcopal fund" which represents our share of the support of the church's executive office. Incidentally, "episcopal" in its primary sense means "pertaining to a Bishop."

(3) Here is the Bishop presiding at a meeting of the district superintendents. A better title for them would be "Junior Bishops" because they are the chief executives for our territory. Our share of the district superintendents' expenses is listed in our budget as "District Fund."

All our contributions toward denominational expenses we might refer to as family obligations. We help toward expenses for delegates to conferences and also toward the general administration fund for the printing of reports, directories, and other publications.

(4) Here is a retired minister. He, along with all other

retired ministers—also the families of deceased ministers—are pension claimants and are supported by a fund to which each church pays a share.
(5) The widows of deceased ministers receive a check to meet the immediate expenses connected with their husbands' funerals. Our share of that money is listed in our budget.
(6) Here is a young minister serving at a church which cannot afford to pay him enough to live on. To meet the minimum salary required in our denomination, all churches contribute a small share.

All these church-at-large expenses, including a small amount to help interdenominational agencies add up this year to $1,875. That total is about $210.50 more than last year. It is based both on a percentage of the pastor's salary and a percentage of the total budget.
(7) Well, that gives you a picture—or several pictures of our obligations to our church family.

NOW we come to the people who keep our *own church* running. Nearly half of our budget goes for salaries—and these are the checks our treasurer writes with the keenest feeling of value received.
(8) No amount of money can pay for the dedication, the talent, the time, the effort, and the hard work which the members of our staff expend for us.

First of all, of course, is our pastor. The forty-hour week is a myth to a minister.
(9) Outside of the sermons and talks he prepares during the year, he is also on call for all kinds of special services such as weddings and (10) baptisms. Our pastor baptized —— persons last year and received —— into the church. He also gives valuable (11) leadership and guidance to all

church organizations and attends dozens of committee meetings throughout the year. Because of his training and experience in counseling, (12) he spends many hours each week helping troubled persons solve their problems.

(13) Our youth program has been developing very rapidly the last few years thanks to the help of our two student assistants. —— works with the Youth Fellowship, planning meetings and recreational programs.

(14) —— and —— handle the program for the Intermediate Youth Fellowship. They both participate in the morning services.

(15) How we would get along without this member of our staff we can't even imagine. This isn't a good picture of our church secretary, but we had great difficulty getting her to sit still long enough to get any kind of a picture.

One of our other valued workers is (16) our custodian. This is only one of the hundreds of tasks he performs. When the bells ring on Sunday morning, you know he is on the job. You know he is on the job when the driveways are cleared of snow, when the meeting rooms are spic and span, and the grass is neatly cut.

(17) The musical program of our church is one of its most outstanding features. Mrs. —— has been our organist for thirty-three years and her faithful service has made it possible for us to maintain the highest musical standards at every service.

(18) No one knows how many hours go into musical training. Here is Mr. —— coaching one of our singers for a part in an anthem. He works faithfully with the senior choir all through the year.

(19) The Finance Committee is glad to report that the salary appropriation for next year has been increased by $900

and is reflected in the salaries of the pastor, the secretary, the youth directors, the pastor's summer substitutes, and special musical talent.

(20) A great deal of the money spent by a church doesn't show. The maintaining of the buildings and property takes a large portion of our budget. The parsonage, for instance, is to have costly repairs made to the chimney next year. The side porch is to be replaced and new gutters must be installed.

(21) The church house is in constant need of attention since it is used by two Sunday school departments, most of the church organizations, and a constant succession of committee meetings. It also houses the church office.

(22) Here is a picture of our church officials in the church house. We took this picture just after they voted to increase the budget. We hope *you* are as happy about it as they are.

(23) The Church itself must be constantly kept in good repair. Here you see the painters at work on the exterior. Next year we shall put $750 into the budget toward repainting the church four years hence.

(24) Each season brings its maintenance problems. Here you see the custodian spreading ashes on an icy pavement so that Sunday worshipers can reach the front door safely.

(25) Here is his assistant operating the lawn mower in the back yard of the parsonage. We hope some day to have a power snowplow to ease the winter work.

(26) Imagine the labor required to get the property back to normal after the Lollypop Fair. It's a wonderful community event for the children, but it takes many weeks to comb the popcorn out of the gravel and nurse the grass back to life.

(27) One of the most beautiful sights in town is the memorial Azalea garden along the Post Road wall. Those plants and all the shrubs and trees on the property require daily attention from the custodian and his helpers.
(28) Well, so far we have looked at our Conference expenses, our salaried staff, and the buildings and grounds which call for constant repairs and maintenance. Let us now have a glimpse of some of the *organizations* in the church and think of *their* place in our church budget.
(29) Here is our faithful and devoted senior choir. Their robes must be kept in good repair and new ones provided as the choir increases in size. Remember also the music which must be purchased for both choirs. Our music budget is very small considering the quality of the work done by the singers.
(30) In the case of the Junior Choir, it is the members themselves who increase in size making constant replacement of robes necessary. One young man has outgrown two robes this year and is now working on his third.
(31) The material is purchased from the music fund and generous volunteer workers do the sewing.
(32) The buildings are in use all day Sunday and many hours each day throughout the week. Heat, light, water, and gas account for the $1,400 in the budget. Here is the Beginner Department in the comfortable room in the basement of the church house. (33) Another group occupies the room while the parents are attending the church service.
(34) Recreation is an important part of the youth program. The upper church parlor is a hard room to heat—but it must be kept comfortable for all church activities.
(35) Perhaps the temperature can fall a few degrees dur-

ing a basketball game—but the lights are still burning—and there may be a pane of glass or two to replace now and then.

(36) The lower church parlor is the scene of all large organizational meetings and social events. Here is the woman's society in the midst of a mission study meeting. But we hardly need to tell you about the church parlor because you are in it tonight.

(37) For two years, the couples' club took entire charge of the rehabilitation of the church house—and then enjoyed a midnight snack afterwards. But now that all the major work has been done, the constant week-to-week expenses are included in the church budget.

(38) Our church is used not only by our own organizations but also by community groups such as the Camp Fire Girls, (39) the Girl Scouts, (40) the Boy Scouts and Cub Scouts, Alcoholics Anonymous, and many others. We are glad to make all these groups feel at home—and we don't mind at all if the light, heat, and repair bills show the effect of this community service at the end of the year.

(41) Now we have a few pictures left of what some of us feel are among the most important items in the budget. Our benevolence giving. . . . The help we give other people both in this country and abroad.

You will see a brown booklet in your folder, entitled "CROWDED OUT?" and it describes the church building programs which will take place in our vicinity the next two years. Some poor, rural congregations raise all the money they can through hard sacrifice—but they need help to provide an adequate place for worship. The Conference is raising $200,000 to help these needy congregations and our share this year is $850. It will help churches like this one.

(42) One of the other projects our hearts are in is the Casa Materna orphanage in Naples, Italy. Here is a picture of the children at Casa Materna. (43) They were rescued from living quarters like this and are being cared for with meager funds provided by churches like ours—churches with a heart. (44) This is what the orphanage looks like. We'll see more of these children before the evening is over. Our benevolence budget has been increased by nearly $1,805 for next year.

(45) Well, that's part of the story in pictures and surely you can see the life surging through this building as you think of it in terms of its people. In case you want to know who has been doing all of this talking—

(46) *I* have. And I hope this story will make a difference in your church giving for next year.

Housekeeping and Utilities

Imagination is needed to visualize the second part of the program. The room is darkened and high on a platform at the front a miniature church is placed against a black curtain. This church happens to have a scale-model of its building about three feet long, but any small church can be used—even the kind that is placed in a toy village under a Christmas tree.

At the side of the room concealed by a curtain is a helper ready to provide sound effects as the script is read. He will need a vacuum cleaner, a toy piano (unless he is near a real one), a hammer, and a telephone bell. Some electrical equipment must be installed ahead of time, as will be seen from the script. It is necessary that the sound effects be timed perfectly for the success of this part of the program.

After a two-minute announcement from the dinner chairman, a narrator reads as follows:

What do you think of first when you see a church?

Sermons? Prayers? Music? Certainly you do!

But it may be a surprise to you to find out how many other things there are to think about . . . things like soap powder, moths in the carpet, bookshelves, light bulbs, dish towels, floor wax.

After all, if we didn't spend money on good housekeeping, your church wouldn't be a fit place to hear sermons and prayers and music.

Speaking of *hearing*, do you know this sound is heard every day in church? . . . (*sound of vacuum cleaner*). . . . Sounds like we need a new one! For extra custodial service we are spending $600 next year, an increase of $450.

Do you ever look at our church and say a prayer that it will never be damaged by wind or lightning or fire? Here's a danger signal we hope we'll never see . . . (*red lights flash in small church*) . . . but we must be insured against it. Our insurance costs have gone up from $800 to $1,300 for next year. But we now feel we're very well protected.

We were talking about sounds a minute ago. Do you know what this means? . . . (*sound of piano being tuned*). . . . It means the piano tuner is here. We have five pianos which have to be tuned and repaired in addition to the work done on the organ. Our bill for that is $100 a year.

You wouldn't stay long in a cold church in the wintertime. Ours is always nice and warm. Do you know what it means when you see *this* against the sky? (*smoke comes out of chimney*) It means the heat's on and we're all ready for a service or a meeting. We hope our fuel bill won't be more than $1,000 next year.

When we have a clean, comfortable church—then we want to let our people know what's going on. Our monthly magazine, our letters, and our printed bulletins help tell the story. We plan to spend $450 to tell our story next year and we hope it will lead all our members and friends right through the front door . . . (*Spotlight is turned on samples of printed materials pinned to black curtain*). . . .

And suppose you came in the front door and the church was dark? You'd say, "Let's turn on the lights!" If the treasurer has paid the light bill and all the bulbs are working, then our church will look like this! . . . (*lights on in church*). . . . Lights and gas and water will cost $400 next year.

One very important thing is missing in this good housekeeping bill. Do you know what this sound means? . . . (*sound of hammering*). . . . In a church as old as ours, there's always a loose board somewhere or a roof to be repaired or a wall to be patched. Repairs to the building cost $700 a year—and there's always a new crack showing up!

Do you know what sound is heard oftener than any other? Oftener even than the organ? Oftener than the preacher's voice? Listen . . . (*sound of telephone ringing*) . . . then a cheerful voice says, "Methodist Church," and the busy day begins. Our church phone bill is about $350 a year—and it would be very quiet around here if we didn't pay it!

Probably the most noticeable housekeeping item of all is what we pay to keep the outside of the church clean and sparkling . . . (*strong spotlight on church*). . . . Every eye is drawn to it as hundreds of people pass it every day. We are putting aside $750 this year toward the next painting bill.

Remember our housekeeping story!

We're awfully blue when we're in the red. So to keep it white, we need some green to stay in the black!

Minor Items

At this point, some humor is injected into the program in the form of a "poem" read as the treasurer and a group of workers act out a simple pantomime.

The original poem contains names of persons and if a church wishes to adapt it, actual names can replace "treasurer," "finance chairman," "this lady"—as long as the meter remains the same.

As the treasurer sits at a table busily engaged with a small piggy bank, five persons come to him as indicated in the script. Each one receives some money and walks on across the platform and out of sight. Finally, four small choir children approach in their robes—holding one hymn book. The pantomime should be quite agitated here. Their expressions and gestures indicate that they must have more books and the treasurer is distressed to find that the piggy bank is empty.

At the words, "We think it is quite fitting," two choir children reach down from the platform and bring up a big box fancily wrapped in colored crepe paper and a large paper bow. It should be wrapped so that the treasurer can get into it easily. As the last line of the poem is read, out comes a very much larger pig and the treasurer registers great delight.

Here is the "poem":

A Run on the Banker

To run a church as big as ours
We need a lot of people.
We need a painter now and then
To polish up the steeple.

We need our fine musicians
To practice Thursday night.
We need our pastor Sundays
To teach us what is right.

There's one important person
Who's the subject of this rhyme
—And he's our faithful banker
We need him ALL the time!

(Enter Treasurer with Piggy Bank, Sits at Table)

It's he who holds the purse strings,
It's he who shakes the bank;
And when our church is solvent,
We all have him to thank.

He counts the cash on Sunday
A pleasant task indeed!
But first thing Monday morning
There's something that we need.

(Counts Coins and Drops Them in Bank)

How can we paint the woodwork
Until we buy some paint?
We have to do some shopping
Or hear a loud complaint

(Man in Overalls with Empty Paint Can)

From all the willing workers
Who volunteer their time.
They *must* have tools to work with—
So can you spare a dime?

Now what's that constant racket
That everyone can hear?
Our secretary's typing
A million sheets a year!

(Sound of Type-writer)

She uses reams of paper
And stencils by the score.
The treasurer often wonders,
Can he PAY for any more?

(Secretary)

And here's our finance chairman,
He has an annual bill
And once again the treasurer
Dips down into the till.

(Financial Secretary Carrying Box of Envelopes)

How's the money lasting,
The anxious members say?
Think we have sufficient
Until the first of May?

A procession of committees
His daily cares increase.
This lady needs ten dollars
To help the cause of peace.

(Peace Committee Chairman)

And here's another worker
With a need we can't deny.
To decorate the altar
Some flowers she must buy.

(Woman Carrying Empty Vase)

Poor banker has his troubles.
He's out there on a limb.
Every week a pile of bills
Stacks up in front of him.

(Shakes Bank with Worried Look)

Now here's a strange procession,
Whatever can *they* need?
You mean these four choir members
Have just *one book* to read?

(Children in Choir Robes)

We've paid out all our money
There's nothing left in here—
But more will soon be coming
To start another year.

We think it seems quite fitting
Since the treasury is so slim,
That we should thank the banker
And do something nice for him.

(Children Present Large Box)

So here's a handsome present—
And it's very kindly meant.
It's bigger—and it's better
By a full fifteen per cent!

(Opens It and Joyfully Holds Up Big *Piggy Bank)*

World Service

The chairman again makes a two-minute comment on the pantomime while preparations are made for the final portion of the program—a series of skits, also in pantomime, while a fourth narrator reads a script.

The subjects of these skits are of course determined by the uses to which a church's world-wide contributions are put. The items are usually grouped in a budget under a general classification and the church might not be aware of where the money is sent after it reaches the denomination's headquarters.

It is necessary in that case to find out where the church's missionary activity is and to adapt the program accordingly. The final choices for this program were determined by what costumes were available or easily provided to depict the various nationalities.

It is interesting to note that in this particular program, a man who has always opposed giving to the cause of missions found himself cast as one of the missionaries! He remarked later that he had always thought missionaries tried to impose their beliefs on persons of other cultures. "I didn't know they were doctors and teachers and architects," he declared—and promptly made his first pledge to the missionary cause!

Script for World Service Skits

In some ways a church budget is like a vegetable garden. Some of the vegetables grow down deep in the earth and cannot be seen. In our budget some of the items such as utilities, taxes, insurance, interest, denominational expenses—lie under the surface and even though they are vital to the church, they aren't very exciting to think about.

There's something else in our budget that grows above the surface, however . . . something we can actually see and become excited about. That's the money that goes directly to help people . . . to teach them God's Word, to educate them, heal them, clothe and feed them.

"Benevolent" is a wonderful word. It means "kindly," "doing good." The benevolence portion of the budget reflects our "kindliness." It's the good we can do for God's children everywhere.

(Missionary Enters) The term "World Service" means just what it says—service to the world. That service is administered by more than 10,000 trained missionaries supported by our denomination. Who are these people in other parts of the world who need our help? *(Child Enters, Takes Bible from Missionary, Stands at Back)* Here is a child who lives in Greece. She has never seen a Bible. As the result of our benevolent giving, 50,000 New Testaments written in modern Greek were distributed to the people of Greece.

Korea has been in our thoughts for the last few years. We sent our boys to Korea to stem the tide of communism. Now we

(Korean Mother Holding Doll Enters, Takes Items from Missionary and Stands Next to Greek Child)

are sending our dollars to relieve the hunger and destitution that always follow in the wake of war. This young mother is receiving food and clothes for her baby and an army blanket to help keep them warm.

Our dollars are active in the field of Christian education, too. Do you remember Miss Abe, the Japanese student we entertained here last fall? She received a scholarship, as the result of your World Service gifts, which made it possible for her to come to this country to study. She will take her Christian beliefs and training back to Japan to help her people. Scholarships in amounts up to $1,600 are available to these foreign Christian students.

(Japanese Girl Enters, Receives Scholarship, Stands with Others)

A large portion of our "kindliness" giving goes to help schools, churches, and hospitals in Africa and India. Here is an Indian girl, Deena Sonna, who received training in public health at Harvard University. She went back to her native village of Yellary fully educated and equipped with modern instruments and techniques. She arrived there just as a cholera epidemic was raging and went to work to save the lives of hundreds of stricken natives.

(Nurse Enters, Receives Instrument Case from Missionary, Stands with Others)

There is no way to measure the value of the money that goes for these causes. The value of a dollar? It's the value of a life.

(All Off)

Let us also look for a moment at the "kindliness" money we spend in the United States. There are missionaries who serve as teachers, doctors, and technical advisors.

(2nd Missionary Enters)

When we talk about Indians, we are apt to think of Wild West stories on the old frontiers. But there are *343,000 Indians* living in the United States and a large portion of them are of our faith. One of the Indian Missions is located in Lawton, Oklahoma, and part of our World Service giving goes to buy books, paper, and other supplies for the Mission school. The battle against ignorance and illiteracy is the first one we must win in the great crusade for education.

(Two Indians Enter, Receive Books from Missionary)

(Leave)

Our money also goes to the backward sections of the country where medical aid is needed. After all, if Americans are not kept in good health, they cannot benefit from the books and the other supplies we send them. Many people think of missionaries as being only preachers—but there are hundreds of medical doctors in the mission field, not only in distant

(Ragged Mountaineer Enters with Shotgun, Has Arm Bandaged by Doctor)
(Leaves)

parts of the world but in our own country as well. Here is a man from the hills of Tennessee visiting a doctor in one of our mission hospitals.

(Mexican Enters and Looks at Blueprints with Missionary)
(Leaves)

Not only does the church advance the cause of education and give necessary medical aid, it also provides buildings for congregations which have no place to worship. Here is a Mexican whose people have been holding religious services in the back of a store. The blueprints are ready for a church building and a portion of your money will help erect this new church. A large sum of money has gone to help build churches for a Latin-American congregation in Texas, a Filipino congregation in Vallejo, California; and a Mexican congregation in San Jose, California.

(Missionary Off)

It is hard to know where to stop in our benevolent giving. Can we ever say "No" to people who *want* to learn? People who *want* to be healthy? People who *want* to know about Jesus Christ? People who *want* to join a church? There really is no end to it just as there is no end to kindness in the world. If kindness and unselfishness ever die, then our churches will close their doors.

(Old Lady Enters, Sits in Rocker)

We can see the results of SOME of our money much nearer home—in fact right in our own district. Our church has increased its gift from $450 to $660 for next year to help meet the higher costs of maintaining our Home for the Aged. Here is a familiar scene in the Home. In addition to the money we give, our members do many thoughtful things for the Home family. Packages are sent at Christmas time and gifts of food are made from time to time. The residents always enjoy visits from church friends and every thoughtful deed reminds them that they have not been forgotten.

(Friend Enters Gives Packages)

(Makes Old Lady Comfortable; Fixes Shawl on Foot Stool, Passes Candy)

This old lady will now be much happier because of the generosity of our church. The visitor represents our benevolent gifts. And she has added something even more valuable—the personal touch which really makes a gift live. Before she returns home she will help her aged friend out to the yard where she can enjoy the Springtime garden.

(Visitor Helps Old Lady Out)

Is there anyone in our church who does not know what Casa Materna means? Is there anyone who does not know about Dr. Santi and his wife who took two destitute children into their home in Naples,

Italy, fifty years ago when they had barely enough food for their own family? They went on taking in hungry, homeless waifs and today, thanks to the help of kindly Christian people, they are housing, educating, and loving 500 children.

(Two Children Enter)

We know more about Casa Materna than we used to because one of our members is serving there this year.

(Two More Children Enter)

We can see the Casa Materna orphanage through his letters. We know it is a thrilling day when a box arrives from our church.

(Two More)

"The things you sent were wonderful," he writes. "Everyone was so excited. You should have seen the way they received the shirts and toys . . . like they were made of gold. . . ."

(Two More)

(Missionary Brings Box, Children Open It, Take Out Toys, Clothes, Act Very Happy)

And another time, he tells us about little Vincenzo. "The other day I noticed he had no socks so I bought him three pairs and now he wears one pair and carries the others around with him. I am giving Vincenzo his things a little at a time. He gets kind of confused if he gets too much at once. If you could only see how much these children appreciate the help the

> church is giving them, it would make you glow inside. . . ."
>
> That is a wonderful phrase: "It makes you glow inside."
>
> Our giving to our own church—which is really a gift to ourselves—is necessary and we do it with pleasure; but the part of our giving that goes to others, to people like you have seen tonight, that's the giving that "makes us glow inside."

When the program was over, the chairman gave an enthusiastic three-minute talk, stating that the program had left little doubt about the church's need for a higher budget. He urged everyone "while the inspiration of this close-up view of our church is still fresh in your minds" to fill out their pledge cards prayerfully, thoughtfully, and generously. He pointed to posters on the walls which listed various categories of giving indicating what a fifteen per cent increase would mean. For instance, $1 becomes $1.15; $1.50 becomes $1.73; $5 becomes $5.75.

When the cards had been signed, baskets were passed to receive them and the doxology was sung. The dinner had been served promptly at 7:00 P.M. and the "Amen" of the benediction was heard at exactly 9:30.

Of the pledge cards signed that night, eighty-seven per cent were either increased or new pledges. The total amount pledged was thirty per cent more than had been pledged by the same persons the preceding year!

The evening was over for everyone but the members of the finance committee. They sat down to compile a list of the persons who had not attended the dinner because a letter was to be mailed to them the next morning in preparation for calls which would be made the following Sunday to complete the campaign.

The text of the letter follows:

Dear friend:

We believe straight talk will do it.

WE WANT to increase salaries—by $900.

WE HAVE to increase our insurance—by $500.

WE OUGHT to increase our benevolent gifts—by $1,800.

WE NEED more supplies—$525 more.

WE HAVE VOTED to spend $500 on emergency building improvements.

WE MUST pay more for supplies—$520 more.

All that adds up to $4,745 more than this year's church budget. THAT'S THE BEST NEWS WE CAN POSSIBLY GIVE YOU. It means our church is alive and growing. If it were dead or dying—the budget would decrease or stay the same year after year.

To meet this fifteen per cent increase in the budget, we are making an earnest appeal to you to increase your gift to the church by fifteen per cent.

What does a fifteen per cent increase look like?

$ .50	becomes	$ .57	3.50	becomes	4.03
1.00	becomes	1.15	4.00	becomes	4.60
1.50	becomes	1.73	5.00	becomes	5.75
2.00	becomes	2.30	7.00	becomes	8.05
3.00	becomes	3.45			

We missed receiving your pledge at the dinner last night—but as has been the custom in other years, teams of men will go out Sunday afternoon—and we hope you will receive your callers with enthusiasm and generosity. If you have never signed a pledge card before—we urge you to do so this year and thereby take the question mark out of the church's plan for 1954–55.

REMEMBER—THE CHURCH HAS NO MONEY BUT OURS.

THE FINANCE COMMITTEE.

The final tabulation after the Sunday canvass revealed that 146 persons had increased their pledges for a total of $13,889; and sixty-four new pledges had been obtained totaling $2,646.

Toward the budget of $27,600, the amount needed in pledges was $22,620. (The balance was to be made up from plate collections, organization gifts, and special holiday offerings.)

The actual amount pledged was $23,728. The church, therefore, soared over its goal by $1,108!

The finance committee had made the mistake of underestimating the response the congregation would make to such a program. The error was rectified the following year, however, when $5,000 was added to the budget for a director of religious education. Again the budget was oversubscribed.

Lest anyone think there is a feeling of satisfaction or smugness among the people, let us point out that the congregation is still far below what the minister and the leaders are sure can be accomplished. The number of persons who do not pledge is far too high. The level of giving is far too low. The spirit of stewardship has not yet taken real possession of the people. So there is always a mounting goal—always a new challenge to their spirits as well as to their pocketbooks.

Many churches are educating their people to give a proportionate share of their income and that is one way of developing a feeling that one's support of one's church should be substantial, that it should be *felt*. One church has suggested the following table as a guide:

*Net Income Subject to Tax	Your Pledge Should Range From 2% to 5%
$ 5,000	$ 100 to $ 250
6,000	120 to 300
7,000	140 to 350
8,000	160 to 400
9,000	180 to 450
10,000	200 to 500
12,000	240 to 600
14,000	280 to 700
15,000	300 to 750
16,000	320 to 800
17,000	340 to 850
18,000	360 to 900
20,000	400 to 1000
25,000	500 to 1250
30,000	600 to 1500
35,000	700 to 1750
40,000	800 to 2000
45,000	900 to 2250
50,000	1000 to 2500

* Table approved by Certified Public Accountants

This chart gives the picture on a weekly basis with a strong emphasis on the tithe or ten per cent gift.

Weekly Income	3%	4%	5%	6%	7%	8%	9%	Tithe	15%	20%
$ 50.00	$1.50	$2.00	$2.50	$3.00	$3.50	$4.00	$4.50	$5.00	$7.50	$10.00
$ 75.00	2.25	3.00	3.75	4.50	5.25	6.00	6.75	7.50	11.25	15.00
$100.00	3.00	4.00	5.00	6.00	7.00	8.00	9.00	10.00	15.00	20.00
$150.00	4.50	6.00	7.50	9.00	10.50	12.00	13.50	15.00	22.50	30.00
$200.00	6.00	8.00	10.00	12.00	14.00	16.00	18.00	20.00	30.00	40.00
$250.00	7.50	10.00	12.50	15.00	17.50	20.00	22.50	25.00	37.50	50.00
$300.00	9.00	12.00	15.00	18.00	21.00	24.00	27.00	30.00	45.00	60.00

The leaflet is called "Pledge Calculator" and is obtainable in quantities from the United Church Canvass, an agency of the National Council of Churches.

Fund raisers are having increasing success with a procedure which church workers shied away from for many years: the guiding of a person in his decision about how much to give.

In the case of building fund campaigns as well as budget drives, this approach is made with great tact and after careful study of the possible resources and the personality of the prospect. When the matter is well-handled, the giver, instead of resenting the suggestion is pleased that he has been considered in so high a bracket. Often a man who has thought of giving $100 finds himself thinking seriously in terms of $1,000 when callers in his general income bracket who themselves expect to give that much express their hope that he might like to join others at that level of giving.

The increasing popularity of the eight-step Sector Plan originated by the American Baptist Convention testifies to the efficacy of that procedure, also to the wisdom of central training sessions for workers in a specified territory or sector. The group training and the sharing of materials and literature lead also to the sharing of faith and enthusiasm.

Increases in church pledges as a result of the use of the Sector Plan have been reported as high as 525 per cent in one year. In a territory in Vermont and northeastern New York State the annual giving in fifty-five churches increased from $500,064 to $805,683 or sixty-one per cent.

The Rev. William J. Cook gives a detailed description of the Sector Plan in the August, 1955, issue of *Zion's*

Herald and his article includes this significant paragraph:

"Increased finances is not the only fruit of the Sector Project. Every church following the plan faithfully reports a tremendous increase in attendance and interest in all areas of church life, and particularly in the Sunday morning worship service."

Chapter VII

The Public Relations Committee

Frequent reference has been made in these pages to the church public relations committee and it may be optimistic to assume that every church has one.

As the vital function of a public relations program is understood, however, it must surely be seen that such a committee should take its place among the most significant groups in a church. It should be considered not only as the means of implementing a church program, but also as a necessary factor in the formulation of church policy and the organization of the over-all program. Ample allowance should be made in the budget for the effective operation of the committee. In Trinity Methodist Church in Albany, N. Y., $6,635 was allotted to the public relations committee for 1956 out of a total budget of $89,717—more than seven per cent. Of that amount, $1,400 is spent on the air ministry of the church.

The following guide to the personnel and function of such a committee should be considered for even a minimum program:

GENERAL CHAIRMAN

Sees that each organization has a publicity chairman.

Keeps calendar of events and checks each organization

publicity chairman to see that advance and follow-up stories go to newspapers concerning every event.

Outlines function of each sub-committee chairman and sees that each one does his job.

Watches church at each point of contact with public, noting impression made by signs, buildings, property, ushers, music, order of service. Consults with pastor and church committee involved when a flaw is detected.

SUB-COMMITTEE CHAIRMEN

Organization Publicity Chairmen

Write advance and follow-up releases on meetings, parties, committee sessions of each organization.

Send for pictures and biographies of guest speakers.

Provide news for parish paper.

Church Publicity Chairman

Works independently of organization publicity chairmen.

Covers general church events for which no organization is responsible: special services, fund raising publicity, news about the minister, elections, and appointments of church officials, board action, building improvements etc.

Sends special stories to denominational magazines.

Radio and TV Chairman

Makes contacts with station managers and broadcasting division of local council of churches.

Plans and produces programs.

Publications Chairman

Supervises writing and editing of all printing and mimeographing.

Obtains advertising for parish paper.

Provides and distributes pew-rack material.

Historian

Keeps scrapbook of newspaper clippings and files church publications.

Records activities of committee.

Chapter VIII

Here's Your Story

The following pages contain sample news stories on various church events which a publicity writer is at liberty to adapt to his own purposes or use in any way he pleases.

Before you write the author to say, "Your model stories aren't very good because our editor has rewritten every one I have sent him," remember four important things:

1. It is the privilege of an editor to rewrite, cut, or condense any material that comes to him. Most papers do it as a matter of course to avoid the chance of duplicating the story as it appears in some other paper.
2. Newspapers differ widely in journalistic style.
3. How much of a story a paper can use depends upon the space available on a given day.
4. Editors' judgment may differ from ours. Indeed they may differ among themselves—as was seen in the three stories from Marblehead on Page 65.

Consecration of a Building

The new $170,000 addition to the First Church at Pine and Grove Streets will be formally consecrated Sunday, March 6, at 11:00 A. M. by Bishop John Wesley Stewart.

It will mark Bishop Stewart's first visit to the parish since 1953.

Ground for the new wing was broken last April and the structure was completed two weeks ago. It contains eight classrooms, a gymnasium, a social hall, and kitchen facilities. It will be used for the primary, junior, and intermediate departments of the church school and for organization meetings.

Quarters in the rear of the church, formerly used by the Sunday school, have been redecorated to serve as offices for the church staff.

Bishop Stewart will preach on the subject, "Except the Lord Buildeth," and will conduct the consecration service with the assistance of the Rev. Joseph Campbell, pastor.

A reception for Bishop Stewart will follow the service and members of the congregation will have the opportunity to inspect the new wing.

Appointment of New Minister

The Rev. James E. Foster, pastor for the last six years of the First Methodist Church in Larchmont, N. Y., has been named minister of St. Paul's Church in Bridgeport, Connecticut, it was announced today by Bishop Harold Lambert. He succeeds the Rev. Elmer Jones who was recently transferred to Omaha, Nebraska.

Dr. Foster was born in 1910 in Los Angeles, California, and was educated at Ohio State University and Union Theological Seminary. He holds a doctor of philosophy degree from Columbia University and has also done graduate work at Yale Divinity School.

He has traveled extensively in the Far East and is the author of several books on the work of the church in Japan and Korea. He also writes frequently for religious and secular periodicals.

He was ordained in 1939 and served during World War II as a chaplain with the United States Air Forces in the Mediterranean Theater.

Before his pastorate at the Larchmont church, he served churches in Columbus, Ohio; Austin, Texas; and Brooklyn, New York.

Dr. Foster is married to the former Dorothy Johnson and they have two children: Mark, nine; and Dorothy, six. He will preach his first sermon at St. Paul's Sept. 9 and the parish will honor him at a reception following the service.

Seasonal Service

Easter Day will be heralded by St. Peter's Episcopal Church with a 6:00 A. M. dawn service on the church lawn, it was announced today by the Rev. Donald Martin, rector.

Three choirs will participate and a trio of Sunday school children will accompany the congregational singing on cornets. Dr. Martin will deliver a brief message followed by a processional into the sanctuary for the administration of Holy Communion.

The sermon topic at the 11:00 A. M. service will be "He Is Risen." Soloists at the morning service will be. . . . Easter music by the senior choir under the direction of John Bradley will include . . . (titles and composers of anthems).

The altar will be banked with memorial lilies arranged by the following members of the Altar Guild: . . . .

At 4:00 P. M., Sunday school children will present their annual Easter program in the sanctuary under the direction of Mrs. Paul Brown. The following children will participate: . . . .

Organization Election

Howard A. Peters, a trustee and member of the Board of Stewards of Christ Church, was elected president of the Men's Club last night at the annual meeting in the parish house. He succeeds John Marshall who had served for four years.

Also on the new slate are Henry Miller, vice president; Harvey Wilkins, secretary; and Daniel Jenkins, treasurer.

The meeting followed a dinner served by the entertainment committee headed by Mr. Miller assisted by. . . .

James A. Howard described his recent trip to Alaska and showed colored slides to illustrate his talk. He visited several churches in Alaska and inspected the site for a new college to be constructed near Anchorage.

Lewis Holmes, chairman of the program committee, announced that Dr. Brian Donovon, superintendent of schools, will be the speaker at the next meeting June 7. Dr. Donovon will outline the guidance program at the high school and describe ways in which business and professional men in the community can implement the new adult education plans at the school.

A gift was presented Mr. Marshall, the outgoing president, and Mr. Peters paid tribute to his service to the organization.

Anniversary of a Church

A week's celebration of its 100th anniversary is being planned by Christ Methodist Church, Broadway and Fifth Street, Long Island City.

The observance will begin Nov. 2 at 11:00 A. M. with a sermon by the Rev. Harrison Barry, district superintendent. The new organ will be dedicated at 4:00 P. M. followed by a reception to honor Mr. and Mrs. James Beck, donors of the organ.

Honor will be paid Nov. 4 to those who have been members of the church for fifty years. A dinner will be held at 6:00 P. M. in the church parlor followed by a historical pageant under the direction of Mrs. Herbert Schoen. Former pastors and members who have moved away from the community will be invited to return for the occasion.

The Women's Society meeting Nov. 7 at 3:00 P. M. will feature an exhibit of historical items and a talk by Mrs. Schoen on the high points in the history of the church.

The festivities will close Nov. 9 with a centennial address by Bishop John L. Peters.

The congregation was organized Nov. 9, 1856, and the present building was constructed in the winter of that year. It has been renovated twice since then, the first time in 1895 when one wing was partially destroyed by fire, and the second time in 1925 when the building underwent extensive repairs and modernization.

The church has been served by fourteen ministers, six of whom are still living and are expected to attend the centennial celebration.

(This story is what is known as a round-up. Each event

will be the subject of a separate story with full details before Nov. 2.)

Television Program

(This story illustrates how a story which is non-local in origin can be localized.)

The attention of Episcopalians in this vicinity is being called by the Rev. Edgar L. Holmes, rector of Holy Trinity Church, to a weekly series of television broadcasts by the Rev. George P. Adams, assistant executive secretary of the Board of Missions.

The series will appear Saturdays from 1:30 to 2:00 P. M. on Channel 4 beginning Jan. 28.

(Information about the program may be copied from the release sent out by church headquarters.)

Building Improvement

Repairs to the roof of the Trinity Church parsonage will be undertaken shortly as a result of action taken last night at a meeting of the Official Board, it was announced today by Robert Seymour, chairman of the property committee.

(In a large community, the address of the church should be included.)

New Soloist

John Pearson of Tulsa, Okla., tenor soloist for four years with the Tulsa Oratorio Society, has become a member of the choir at the First Presbyterian Church, according to an announcement by Mrs. Kenneth Beers, chairman of the music committee. He is a graduate of the Juilliard School of Music in New York City and has made frequent radio and television appearances. He will make his first appearance with the choir May 19.

Sunday School Opening

All departments of the Sunday school at Trinity Church will hold their first sessions of the season tomorrow at 9:30 A. M.

Registration of new pupils will take place in the church office between 9:15 and 9:30.

Edward L. Stanton, superintendent, has announced the addition of five new teachers to the staff. They are Mrs. R. E. Morrow and Miss Edith Allen, nursery department; Thomas Green, junior department; Mrs. Alice McDermott, intermediate department; and Miss Grace Ladd, senior department.

Last year's enrollment totaled 260, Mr. Stanton points out, and the figure this year is expected to be considerably higher because of new building developments in the community.

The kindergarten room has been repainted and new chairs have been purchased for two classrooms in the junior department.

Members of the teaching staff who are returning for the new year are. . . .

Christmas Parties

A series of Christmas parties will be held Tuesday at the Congregational Church for the children of the church school.

Santa Claus will be the guest of honor at the beginners' party at 1:30 P. M. in the social hall. Mrs. John Clawson is in charge of the program which will include games, entertainment, and the distribution of gifts.

The party for the primary pupils will be held at 2:30 P. M. in the same room and Santa Claus is expected to remain for a special greeting to them. Mrs. Avery Lockwood and a committee of teachers have planned the program.

The juniors and intermediates have planned a joint celebration at 4:00 P. M. with their mothers as guests. Refreshments will include hot chocolate and Christmas cookies made by the children. A program of Christmas carols will be presented by the youth choir.

The senior department party will be held at 8:00 P. M. with Miss Grace Clark and John Enright in charge. A skit entitled "Santa's Ride Home" will be presented with the following students in the cast: . . . .

Pastor's Anniversary

The Rev. Carl A. MacDonald will celebrate his twentieth anniversary as pastor of St. John's Church on April 24. The congregation will observe the occasion with a dinner in the parish hall.

Dr. MacDonald came here after a three-year pastorate at Trinity Church, Bloomington, Illinois, and in two decades has tripled the membership of the church.

Under his leadership, a new church was constructed in 1948 and plans are now under way for an addition to the building to provide more space for the church school.

In addition to his church duties, Dr. MacDonald has taken an active interest in community affairs. He headed the Red Cross fund drive for two years and is a former president of the Rotary Club.

He attended graduate school from 1948 to 1953 earning his master's and doctor of philosophy degrees. He has written two books, "———" during his pastorate here.

A testimonial dinner is planned by the Rotary Club for April 29.

Guest Speaker

Dr. Arthur P. Simon of Yates University will address the Men's Club of Holy Cross Episcopal Church, Main Street and Sutton Avenue, Oct. 30, at 8:00 P. M. on the subject, "Religion in the Atomic Age."

Dr. Simon is professor of Biblical Literature and the author of "Classroom Religion." He is a graduate of the University of Utah and General Theological Seminary and formerly taught at the University of Pennsylvania.

He will be introduced by John Snider, program chairman.

The meeting will also include the installation of officers and a report on the club's current bowling tournament.

Gerald Harding, president, will conduct the meeting and the Rev. Donald Allison, rector, will install the officers. A social hour and refreshments will follow the meeting.

Special Observance

(Another example of the localization of a church-wide event.)

The Petersville Methodist Church will participate Feb. 9 with Methodist churches all over the world in observance of the Week of Dedication, the annual recognition of the church's missionary activity.

The Rev. Lester M. Dawson, pastor, will preach on the topic, "The Church at the Center," and a special offering will be taken for special mission projects.

Among the beneficiaries of the Week of Dedication contributions are the Methodist Committee for Overseas Relief, the Casa Materna Orphanage in Naples, Italy, the scholarship fund for foreign students. . . .

(Follow with information about the Week of Dedication provided by general church headquarters.)

Trustee Election

Elmer Sutherland of 420 Seventh Avenue was elected last night a trustee of the Madison Avenue Presbyterian Church to succeed Marshall Small who has retired after twelve years' service.

Carter Bates and Harvey Smith were reelected to succeed themselves for three-year terms.

Mr. Sutherland is the former church school superintendent and conducted the annual budget drives in 1954 and 1955.

Panel Discussion

To live harmoniously with one's parents, one must first understand them, was the conclusion last night of a panel discussion by four teen-agers at a meeting of the Youth Fellowship at the First Presbyterian Church.

Panel members were Marjorie Jones, Jack Parker, Linda Warner, and Edwin Sullivan, Jr., with the Rev. Sanford Bliss, assistant minister, as the moderator.

Discussing the subject, "What's Right With Our Parents?" the panel analyzed problems which tend to disrupt home life, expressing their own and their parents' points of view.

In summing up the discussion, Rev. Mr. Bliss stated that the collective opinion indicated that mutual understanding results from frank and calm consideration of every conflict which arises between parents and children.

At a business meeting preceding the program, members voted to contribute ten dollars to the church toward custodial services in the recreation room.

Luther Grant and Ann Jacobson were welcomed as new members.

Brief Items

Pastor at Conference

The Rev. Joseph Bergen, pastor of the Greene Street Methodist Church, is in Hartford, Connecticut, this week attending the annual session of the New York East Methodist Conference. He will present a report as chairman of the Conference Board of Missions.

Delegates at Institute

Two members of St. John's Lutheran Church have been named delegates to the Summer Youth Training Institute at Lake George, New York. They are Samuel Davis and Robert Morris. They will leave July 11 and return July 18.

Showing of Film

The motion picture, "Martin Luther," will be shown Tuesday at 8:00 P. M. at St. John's Lutheran Church by the Ladies' Aid. Invitations have been sent to other churches in the community and a large attendance is expected. Proceeds from a free will offering will benefit the scholarship fund of the society. Mrs. Dwight Ackerman is in charge of arrangements.

Committee Appointed

A committee has been appointed at the Fairview Baptist Church to study the interior of the church and make recommendations for redecorating it. The members are. . . .

CONCLUSION

When a reader is bombarded with practical suggestions on mundane matters, it is possible to lose sight of the ultimate goal toward which all church workers are striving.

The color of an usher's suit, a soprano who can't hit the high note, a misspelled word in a bulletin, a faltering financial program, a rusted sign, late newspaper copy—all these factors may seem trivial or significant depending upon one's evaluation of their importance to the total program of the church.

But let us remember that the purpose of good public relations is first to draw people into the church and then to smooth the way for the direct passage of the spirit of God into their lives.

We might consider that Jesus was talking to the churches when He said, "You are the light of the world. A city set on a hill cannot be hid."

Let us set our churches on a hill and place a brightly shining light in every polished window.

Mimeographing the Bulletin

Mimeographing the Bulletin

First step—getting a good stencil

"Church bulletin" stencils are made especially for this need. Three manufacturers recommend the following stencils for best results on their machines:

SPEED-O-PRINT—Church Bulletin Stencil No. 850-CB1
A.B. DICK—Four-page Folder Stencil No. 960-L-1119
HEYER—Church Bulletin Stencil No. 2103-C

Your stencils should be stored at normal room temperatures—not too hot and not too cold. If you keep them near heat, they may melt and stick to their backing sheets. If you keep them in a cold place, they will get brittle, and you will find they are hard to type on.

Second step—cleaning your typewriter

Good stencils come from clean typewriters, so make sure the type on your machine is clean. Also see that the roller is in good condition—not worn uneven or hardened with age.

Third step—getting your stencil ready

You can easily see how much space the copy will take if you type your material beforehand on the inside of one of the bulletins or a piece of paper the same size, ruled like the top printing on the stencil. Stay within these boundaries as you type, and the material will appear as it would on the stencil.

When you have completed your layout, place it beneath the stencil and mark the location of paragraph beginnings and the like with a small dot on the stencil. Now you are ready to cut your stencil.

Fourth step—cutting your stencil

Insert the right edge of the stencil in an envelope or piece of folded paper and feed it into your typewriter. Then disconnect or remove the ribbon and type with an even pressure on the keys. You will need to hit the heavier letters such as the capital "M" and "W" with a little more force. However, use a minimum amount of periods or dots as these form small pools of ink when duplicated and, because they dry slowly, are apt to smear and show through. If you make a mistake, you can correct it by applying correction fluid and then retyping the correct letter or word.

A "cushion sheet" placed against the stencil with the smooth side up will enable your typewriter to cut deeper into the stencil, making a clean-cut letter when it is duplicated. The white surface of the cushion sheet also makes it easier for you to read what you have typed, and you can quickly catch any errors you have made.

You will find that pliofilm or cellophane is sometimes used over the top of stencils. This eliminates cut-out letters, type cleaning during cutting, and swelling of the roller. These stencils may be purchased from some of the stencil manufacturers.

Fifth step—using the right ink

Your machine—its type cylinder, its speed, and other features—will determine what ink should be used for the best results. In general, however, use the best quality quick-drying ink which is suitable for your duplicator. Cheap inks usually contain an inferior grade of lampblack. They also usually have an excessive amount of oil. Such an ink will require you to ink the cylinder more often. It will also give fewer copies per pound of ink, and there will be greater show-through and undesirable offset because of its slow drying.

The three manufacturers recommend the following inks for best results on their machines:

SPEED-O-PRINT—Sovereign Grade A No. 50 Dri-Fast Duplicator Ink. This ink is specially made to bring offsetting and show-through down to a minimum. The ink flows freely and dries quickly. In addition it makes sharp, clean-cut copies in rich black that will not fade or leave an oily outline. It is for use in all open and closed cylinder models and is available in colors.

A.B. DICK—Black Contac-Dri Ink No. 1610. This ink will give excellent results without slip-sheeting (see Step six) because it dries on contact. It has a minimum amount of offset, and there is practically no show-through. It is for closed cylinders only, and it requires a special waxed protective cover for the cylinder.

Black Hardest Ink No. 1764. This ink produces a neat bulletin with very little show-through. It should be slip-sheeted to prevent offset. A waxed cover is necessary for the cylinder, and you may use it on open or closed cylinders.

Black Mimeotone Ink No. 1767. This ink is the best all-purpose ink in an open or closed cylinder. There is only a slight amount of show-through. For best results you should slip-sheet.

HEYER—No. 344 for automatically inked machines; No. 999 for fountain brush-inked machines; Nos. 150 and 151 for hand-inked machines.

Sixth step—running your stencil

It is best to run a dozen or so trial sheets first after you attach the stencil to the cylinder of the duplicator. After you examine these sheets, you can add ink sparingly until all parts of the copy print uniformly clear.

When you have run the first fifty bulletins, brush the ink around in all parts of the cylinder to equalize the ink distribution, but do not add any more ink. When you have run the first 100 copies, add a little ink and brush thoroughly all around, but do not over-ink. Because the ink supply at the top of the page is reduced faster than in other parts, you should exercise extra care to brush the ink well up into the head of the cylinder and the corners. If you repeat this procedure at each fifty or 100 copies, you will avoid the oversupply of ink which frequently causes offset.

After twenty-five copies or less have been run, allow printed sheets to remain in the receiving tray for a few minutes. Then remove them and set them in separate piles. In a very short while evaporation and absorption will make it possible for you to stack the separate piles in one without danger of smudging.

If you use the best quality stencil and ink, there will be very little offsetting—if any—on the printed side of the bulletin. Also, there will be very little show-through. Slip-sheeting will entirely eliminate offsetting.

In slip-sheeting you place a sheet of absorbent paper between the copies as they are printed. You can use the slip-sheets over and over again.

Do not fold your finished sheets until they are perfectly dry. The time it takes for them to dry varies, and you should make a test of one or two sheets before folding them all. In this way you can make sure that there will be no smudging because of the pressure required in folding.

(From *The Methodist Weekly Church Bulletins for 1956*)

Bibliography

Bibliography

Religious Public Relations

Harral, Stewart. *Public Relations for Churches.* New York: Abingdon-Cokesbury, 1945.

Stuber, Stanley. *Public Relations Manual for Churches.* New York: Doubleday & Company, Inc., 1951.

Wolseley, Roland E., *Interpreting the Church Through Press and Radio.* Philadelphia: Muhlenberg Press, 1951.

Religious Publicity and Promotion

Brown, Richard O. *Practical Church Publicity.* Nashville: Broadman Press, 1942.

Brodie, Austin W. *Keeping Your Church in the News.* New York: Fleming H. Revell Company, 1942.

———. *Keeping Your Church Informed.* New York: Fleming H. Revell Company, 1944.

Fortson, John L. *How to Make Friends for Your Church.* New York: Association Press, 1943.

Gilbert, Ralph V. *The Church and Printer's Ink.* New York: Fleming H. Revell Company, 1925. (Out of print.)

Harral, Stewart. *Patterns of Publicity Copy.* Norman, Oklahoma: University of Oklahoma Press, 1950.

———. *Successful Letters for Churches.* New York: Abingdon-Cokesbury, 1946.

Henry, Carl F. H. *Successful Church Publicity.* Grand Rapids: Zondervan Publishing House, 1943.

Leach, William H. *Church Publicity.* Nashville: Abingdon-Cokesbury, 1929.

Pleuthner, Willard A. *Building Up Your Congregation.* New York: Wilcox & Follett Co., 1950.

———. *More Power for Your Church.* New York: Farrar, Straus & Young, Inc. 1952.

Underwood, Kenneth. *Our Story and How to Tell It.* New York: Home Missions Council, 1943.

Radio and Television

Pamphlets

Radio: Quigley, Harold, *Religious Newscasting.* 10¢.
Schmitz, Charles, *Hints on Religious Music for Radio.* 10¢.
Radio Devotions. 10¢.

Television: Bretz, Rudy, *Religious Television Programming.* 10¢.
Hints for Television Demonstration Programs. Free.

The above pamphlets may be obtained from:
Broadcasting and Film Commission
National Council of Churches
220 Fifth Avenue
New York 1, N.Y.

Books

Basic: Chester & Garrison, *Radio and Television.* New York: Appleton-Century-Crofts, Inc., 1950. $5.00.
Hodapp, William, *The Television Manual.* New York: Farrar, Strauss, 1953. $4.50.

Writing: Crews, Albert, *Professional Radio Writing.* New York: Houghton Mifflin Company, 1946. $5.50; text ed. $4.50.
Greene, Robert S., *Television Writing.* New York: Houghton Mifflin Company, 1952, $3.50.
Bretz, Rudy, *Television Script.*

Production: Crews, Albert, *Radio Production Directing,* New York: Houghton Mifflin Company, 1944. $5.50; text ed. $4.50.
Stasheff, Edward, and Bretz, Rudy, *The Television Program.* New York: A. A. Wyn, Inc., 1951. $4.95.
Hubbell, Richard, *Television Programming and Production.* New York: Rinehart & Company, 1950. $3.50.

The Devotional Talk: Schmitz, Charles H., *Windows Toward God*. New York: Abingdon Press, 1950. $1.25. (Eighty-seven three-minute devotional talks.)

Clarity: Flesch, Rudolph F., *The Art of Plain Talk*. New York: Harper & Brothers, 1946. $2.50.

The Radio Sermon: Atkinson, O'Brien, *How to Make Us Want Your Sermon*. New York: Joseph F. Wagner Inc., 1942. $2.75.

Music: Austin, Arthur, *The Family Book of Favorite Hymns*. New York: Funk & Wagnalls, 1950. $2.95. (The most popular hymns as gleaned from radio surveys and polls.) Sandor, Ralph, *Incidental Music*. New York: Alpha Music, Inc., $2.50. (Mood music.)

Public Taste: Seldes, Gilbert, *The Great Audience*. New York: The Viking Press, 1951. $3.75.

Policy: Siepman, Charles A., *Radio, Television, and Society*. New York: Oxford University Press, 1950. $4.00.

Educational Use: Levinson, W. B., *Teaching Through Radio and Television*. New York: Rinehart & Company, Revised Edition 1952. $4.75.

Broadcasting Helps

Broadcasting Religion, A Manual for Local Use. (Chapters on "Why Broadcast Religion?," "Policy," "Microphone Technique," "Audience Measurement," etc.) $1.50.

Television Do's and Don'ts. (Concerning "Preparation," "Attitude," "Talk," "Microphone Presence," "Camera Presence," "Personal Appearance.") 5¢; $3.00 per 100.

Radio Hints for Ministers. (Suggestions for ministers who broadcast.) 10¢; $1.00 per dozen.

Radio Devotions. (The "How" of devotional programming.) 10¢; $1.00 per dozen.

Religious Music for Radio. (A discussion of music purposes, resources, rights, etc.) 10¢; $1.00 per dozen.

Religious Newscasting. (Methods, variety, resources, ideals, etc., in newscasting.) 10¢; $1.00 per dozen.

Can be obtained from:

National Council of the Churches of Christ
in the United States of America
Broadcasting and Film Division
220 Fifth Avenue
New York 1, N.Y.